40 Acres
and
a Mule

The African-American Guide to
Building Wealth
through Real Estate

Written by

Kevin Riles

Library of Congress Cataloging

Riles, Kevin, 1973-
40 Acres and a Mule: The African American Guide to Building Wealth through Real Estate
Kevin Riles. – 1st ed.
p. cm.

ISBN 978-0-6151-8895-9
1. Real Estate 2. Business 3. African American - Business

To the loves of my life and the women that **MADE** me
and **MAKE** me the man I am today

Parthenia Flannel – My Grandmother

Ava Parker – My Mother

Cher Riles – My Wife and Best Friend

Madison Riles – My Beautiful Daughter and Legacy

Table of Contents

Part 1: How to Get Your First 40 Acres

Preface: Why I Wrote this Book   vi

Chapter 1 - Why 40 Acres and a Mule?   2

Chapter 2 - Real Estate: The Best Way to Build Wealth   11

Chapter 3 - Yes! You *Can* Finance Your 40 Acres   23

Chapter 4 - Putting Your Credit in Order   33

Chapter 5 - Determining How Much House You Can Afford   47

Chapter 6 - Types of Financing Available   62

Chapter 7 - How to Choose a Real Estate Partner   75

Part 2: Building Generational Wealth: How to Turn Your 40 Acres into True Wealth!

Chapter 8 - Investing In More than Just Your 40 Acres   81

Chapter 9 - Types of Real Estate to Look For When Investing   93

Chapter 10 - The 40 Acre Millionaire Maker!!   103

The Last Acre...   112

About Kevin Riles   114

To find out more information about Kevin or to have him speak to your organization on Real Estate, Success and Motivation, please contact his office at the numbers below:

Kevin Riles
2938 South Main
Stafford, TX 77477
Phone: (281) 403-3700
Email: info@kevinriles.com
Website:
http://www.KevinRiles.com

Preface: Why I Wrote this Book

I once asked my mother what she wanted from me. What type of Man did she want me to be? She leaned over and told me, "Kevin, I want you to be a GREAT Man." When I probed her further as to what a great man is, she just told me, " I want you to be great." Years later she gave me a book written by Kirby John Caldwell called the *Gospel of Good Success* and in the inside cover she wrote the scripture reference Psalm 37:23 which reads, "The steps of a good man are ordered by the LORD: and he delighteth in his way."

I wrote this book to continue my quest to be a Good Man and I feel that I was led by God to reveal to Black folks the realities and rewards of real estate ownership. At the time of this writing, African-American households are being decimated due to the foreclosure crisis that is gripping our nation. Unscrupulous lenders and uneducated buyers have combined to make this a dark time in the economic history of our country. The dream of homeownership has become the nightmare of foreclosure for millions of homebuyers and this is disproportionately affecting Black households.

This book is for those African-Americans who want to get an economic foothold in the American Dream. I named the book *40 Acres and a Mule* to remind us that it was a little more than 140 years ago when we were offered not only our freedom but also a financial foundation after 400 years of slavery. Like many promises of that time, 40 acres was never to be. To offer you advice that my mother often gives, "Make a Decision and Live with it." Therefore, today you as a black person in America have to make a decision not to live in the past but to press on toward the future. At no other time in history has it been easier for Black folks to purchase real estate. This book is an attempt to demystify that process. More importantly, it is my attempt to educate you on the benefits of owning real estate. Not only from the typical "Everyone Needs to Own their Own Home" mantra but by really dissecting the concept of passing on Generational wealth.

I hope that you enjoy this book. More importantly, I hope that you will take the axioms you find and apply them to your economic life. Finally, I hope you will agree that I am living up to my mother's wish, that I am a GOOD Man.

Kevin Riles

October 8, 2007

Part 1: How to Get Your First 40 Acres

1

Why 40 Acres and a Mule?
"A good man leaveth an inheritance to his children's children.."
Proverbs 13:22

WAKE UP!!!

I am a big Spike Lee fan! Not only because we graduated from the same school, Morehouse College, but also because he knows how to get his audience's attention. In my favorite movie of his, *School Daze*, there is a scene where one of the characters runs to the middle of the campus and starts to ring the old bell. As he is ringing it he yells at the top of his lungs, "W−A−K--E U--P!! W−A−K--E U--P!! W−A−K--E U--P!!!!!" Spike, through this character, is telling Black folks to wake up to the issues in our community. He is telling them to wake up to our people's problems.

Well, my friend, I am ringing the BELL again. WAKE UP!! WAKE UP!! WAKE UP!! I want you to wake up to the fact that Black folks as a whole are leaving our future generations bankrupt. That's right, bankrupt. Our grandmothers and grandfathers not only fought for us to have equal civil rights but economic rights as well. We seem as a people to get caught up in the civil rights portion and ignore the fact that we have, like no other time in history, an opportunity to gain equal economic rights. With that being said, it is about time for those of us who, like me, have been blessed with knowledge and skills to enlighten the rest. I am convinced that the easiest path to financial prosperity for African-Americans is through real estate. There is no other time in our history where obtaining real estate has been easier and more financially fulfilling.

I love the scripture at the beginning of this chapter: "A good man leaveth an inheritance to his children's children" *Proverbs 13:22*. God's word even tells us that we MUST leave an inheritance to our children and our children's children. That is the word from on high. We are failing our descendants if we do not make God's word true. Our ancestors laid the civil groundwork for us to have the opportunity to make economic strides.

Homeownership is one of the most fundamental desires of all Americans. To be able to live in a house on a piece of land, no matter how big or small, and be called the owner is living the American Dream.

Owning real estate, whether it is for your own personal home or to purchase with the intent of making a profit remains one of the most lucrative investments we can make in these times. More Americans are building wealth through real estate than by any other means and purchasing a home remains the single largest investment a person will make in their lifetime.

That was not always the case for African-Americans, and to some extent, it remains untrue. During the years when African-Americans were slaves to Southern plantation owners, the idea of homeownership for Black folks was a myth. African-Americans were oppressed and prevented from owning anything, even their own lives.

THE ORIGINAL 40 ACRES

Major General William T. Sherman issued Special Field Order #15 on January 16, 1865, stating that compensation would be made to American slave families when they were freed after the Emancipation Proclamation was signed. This meant that, as remuneration for unpaid services to the plantation owners while they were held as slaves, all slave families would receive 40 acres of land--particularly land and plantations that were abandoned and confiscated during the Civil War--and a mule they could use to help work the land. A 30-mile tract of land along the coast between South Carolina and Georgia was the proposed land set aside in Special Field Order #15.

However, once President Abraham Lincoln was assassinated, newly sworn-in President Andrew Johnson vetoed the bill and the property was returned to the white owners, even though the bill had been passed by Congress. For many African-Americans, this move was a step back and one that had them standing still for over 100 years.

Forty years after Martin Luther King gave his legendary address at the March on Washington, things have changed drastically. African-Americans have moved into new territory where building wealth and homeownership is concerned. More and more African-Americans are living the American Dream where once they felt it was *only* a dream.

However, despite these changes, many of us still hold on to the belief that we will never be able to own a home or even worse, build long-lasting wealth.

This is a very sad statistic. Homeownership is something that should be the right of every American and is available to those who take the steps needed to become a homeowner. Education is the biggest obstacle that keeps us from turning the dream of homeownership into reality. An even bigger challenge is believing the notion that we can actually build *wealth* and live like millionaires by investing in real estate.

MY STORY

I'm the perfect example of an African-American who is living the American Dream and building wealth through investing in real estate. I am a 34-year-old Black man who owns close to one million dollars worth of real estate. My story does not begin there, though. I was raised in a single parent household until the age of 13, when my mother married my stepfather. The most instrumental people in my life were my mother and my grandparents who I called Mama and PawPaw. Of the many life lessons my mother taught me, the one that drives me today was her want for me to be, in her words, "A Great Man"--a man that leads his people, a man that is God-fearing and, most importantly, an honest man. She always wanted me to live up to the Bible verse, "The steps of a good man are ordered by the Lord." I have spent the first 34 years of my life attempting to live up to that. This book started as a desire to educate my people of building generational wealth. It's one thing to be rich and wealthy yourself, but to build wealth that your children's children will have is the mark of the highest calling.

Getting back to my story, I am the broker and owner of RE/MAX Upscale Properties in Houston, Texas. I have been a practicing real estate professional for 10 years. Before that, I was a computer project manager at the largest oil company in the world. When I left college, I had dreams and ambitions of being rich, not knowing at that time that being rich is just a temporary state but building wealth is eternal. Most of my clients were and still are African-Americans. I have been shocked over the years not only with the lack of understanding of how to purchase a home, but also with the ignorance of how to use real estate to build wealth that we as a people lack.

I have accomplished a lot in my short life. Since 2005, I have consistently sold over 500 homes per year. At the time of the writing of this book, I am currently the #2 ranked agent in Houston, Texas, out of 10,000 realtors. I am a licensed mortgage broker in the state of Texas. I have originated over 300 loans in my 10 years of owning our mortgage company. I have also recently opened Riles Insurance and Financial Services, a Farmers Insurance Agency. In 2005, I was named the Broad Listing Broker for HUD Foreclosures in Southeast Texas, giving me the responsibility to sell government foreclosures in an 18-county area that includes Houston, Texas, the fourth largest city in the United States.

I list all of these accomplishments not out of glory for myself. I want you, the reader, to know that you are reading a book written by someone who knows what he is talking about. I could tell you that I have a BS in Computer Science from Morehouse College and an MBA in Finance from the University of St. Thomas. However, that would not matter. A person can have all the theoretical knowledge in the world, but if they have not practiced what they are preaching that knowledge is useless.

You see I am also a fourth-generation landowner. Our ancestors were denied choices when it came to owning property. If you look out over the history of the world, land (real estate) ownership was the first predictor of wealth. Only in the last century has the attainment of money become the indicator of wealth. The idea in history was that the wealthy owned land and the poor worked the land. Believe it or not, that principle holds true today. Due the blessing of God and my gene pool, my ancestors were smart enough to know that in order to build generational wealth you must own land. My great-great grandparents were sharecroppers who eventually purchased their own property. That, my friends, is the reason for this book. It is to teach you the time-honored principle of how to build wealth for you, your children, and your children's children.

Through the years, I've met many other African-American investors who've had the desire and determination to move beyond the notion that wealth was beyond them. They courageously embraced the idea that by educating themselves and taking certain steps they could become wealthier than they'd ever imagined through investing in real estate.

Obtaining this wealth is my hope for you and for all African-Americans who have the desire to either own a home of their own or to go beyond that and create a portfolio of real estate that will bring them lasting income beyond what they could ever receive by working a 9-to-5 job. It is possible, and many people have achieved this goal.

I have worked that 9-to-5 job just like you have. I started my professional career working for the largest oil company in the world. Since my undergrad degree is in computer science, my first job out of school was as a Systems Analyst. Simply stated, I HATED THAT JOB! The company was wonderful but I HATED THAT JOB! I realized early on that I wanted more for my life. I wanted to leave a lasting impact on people's lives and developing computer systems was not going to help me reach that goal. It was a chance encounter that got me into real estate and forever changed my life. Even at the age of 23, I knew I wanted to have a million-dollar net worth by the age of 35. That encounter with my real estate mentor, who at that time was in his 30's and already a millionaire many times over, forever changed my definition of wealth and how I saw money. That education led me many years later to write this book.

The key is education, and in this book you will learn what it takes to take that first step to purchase your first home.

You'll then learn what it takes to move beyond your first home to wealth by following my five-year Guaranteed Millionaire Investor Plan.

Will it be easy? No. Nothing that is worth it is ever easy. Is it difficult? No. By following the steps outlined in this book to improve your credit, get yourself organized, and start purchasing real estate, you will see homeownership go from being a dream that is out of reach to being right at your fingertips. All you have to do is reach out and grab it.

2

Real Estate: The Best Way to Build Wealth

"Now, one thing I tell everyone is learn about real estate. Repeat after me: real estate provides the highest returns, the greatest values, and the least risk."
Armstrong Williams

"Kevin, you need to buy a duplex!" That quote is the beginning of my wealth-building. Craig Cassell told me that in October of 1998. I was home, living in Houston with my parents after college. In Atlanta, I had lived the last two years of my college life off campus. I had grown into a man in those two years and a man must have his own place. My mother was cool and understanding of a new "adult" living at home to save money, but I wanted to be a MAN! I was confiding this to some elder Black coworkers at the oil company I worked for, and one of them told me to call Craig. Craig was an engineer at one of the hundreds of chemical plants in Houston. I set up an appointment with him to see what he had to say. My coworker told me that he owned quite a bit of real estate and would be the perfect person for me to talk with.

When I met with Craig the first thing out of his mouth was, "Kevin, you need to purchase a duplex." "Why?" I asked, and then he proceeded to break down why real estate was the fastest way to build wealth in one generation. We will get into the types of real estate and what you should buy later, and I will tell you why he specifically was saying a duplex. However, the most important information he gave was the lesson on why real estate was the best way to build wealth.

While the government giving every Black person who was freed from slavery 40 acres and a mule isn't realistic in this day and age (the reparations question can be covered in another book and another time), that doesn't mean you can't obtain your own 40 acres on your own. Never has there been a time when homeownership and building wealth was as possible for all Americans as it is today.

Unfortunately, many African-Americans are still lagging behind white Americans in homeownership by 26.2 percent. That's a staggering number, and one that can be changed by education and a different way of thinking.

Think about it--for over 400 years African-Americans were slaves to wealthy white landowners. During that time, slaves were not permitted to own anything, much less land or a home they could call their own. Since slavery has ended, we have endured another 100 years of coordinated and uncoordinated efforts to keep us from owning land. However, the biggest obstacle to ownership we as a people have to overcome is lack of education. Either by omission or commission, we have not taken advantage of the many opportunities to educate ourselves on the process of homeownership. What was once thought of as an elusive dream has become more attainable than ever before. While the government is not going to hand out 40 acres to every African-American as once promised by General Sherman, all African-Americans can get a homeownership slice of the pie by taking the right steps to get there.

These steps are not unreachable. In addition, as you read through this book and see my step-by-step process to build wealth through homeownership, you'll see that homeownership is right at your fingertips. All you have to do is be determined to make the change and be committed to taking the steps necessary until you have reached your goal.

WHY IS REAL ESTATE THE BEST INVESTMENT?

I am going to answer that question like my grandmother and mother used to tell me when I asked a question (I am sure yours did also): "Because I SAID SO!!" No, I'm just kidding; I would love for the answer to "why real estate" to be that simple. There are many reasons why land ownership has consistently outperformed other investment vehicles over history. There are many wonderful investments that people can participate in, but unlike renting an apartment or home, owning real estate offers a way for people to build equity over time. Now I can say real estate is the best investment out there but let's look at the real deal. Like Cuba Gooding said in *Jerry McGuire*, SHOW ME THE MONEY!!!

In 1963, a two-family home in Boston sold for approximately $7,000. Forty years later, that same home is paid off and worth more than $500,000. That is a return on your investment of over 7,000%! Another example: in 1998 I purchased that duplex I mentioned at the beginning of this chapter for $88,000. Because I purchased in an area that was close to downtown Houston (yes it was the hood when I purchased) and going through a revitalization, I was able to sell that duplex three years later for $150,000. That's a net profit of over $60,000 in three years. That one purchase alone changed the course of my economic life. I was able to start my business and purchase a new, bigger, and better home from that one transaction alone.

Let's take that one step further. Since both my home and the Boston home were duplexes (two-family homes), the first-floor apartments could be rented out for a competitive rent. In both examples, not only did the rent from the apartments cover the mortgage, but it also paid for part of the taxes and insurance as well, allowing myself and the Boston owner to live in the home virtually free! That was money in our pockets.

Over time, inflation allowed for an increase of the rental rates so that over a period of several years the first-floor apartment was actually bringing in more money than what was owed on a monthly basis to carry the house. That excess money from the rent is called cash flow and it is money in the owner's pocket every month to use as the owner sees fit. The owner can use that money to reinvest in the home for upkeep and repairs, put the money in the bank to collect interest, reinvest in other investments such as stocks and bonds or more real estate, or the owner can simply spend that money in any way he or she wishes.

The difference between renting a home and owning it is that when you own it, your monthly payment toward your home is working for you. Owning real estate and paying your mortgage are akin to burning a candle at both ends — in a good way. On one end, you are paying down the debt of the mortgage. Since a mortgage has a fixed number of payments, each time you make a payment you are chipping away at what you owe. On the other end of the candle, you have appreciation, which is the rising in value of your property.

Even if you don't own a duplex that allows for rental

income on a monthly basis, your single-family home is still building equity that you can use later on down the road as you please. You can't do that when you are giving your money each month to a landlord.

It is not how much money you make at the end of the month, it what's you do with your money that makes the difference in how you can use money to build wealth. I'll show you that even with just a little bit of money, you can purchase a home of your own and begin building equity. As time goes on, you will also be able to stretch beyond the home you live in to invest in other properties that will help build wealth.

So let's get into the details of why real estate is the BEST investment for you and your money over time. There are three different factors in investing in real estate that help you accumulate wealth. They are **appreciation**, **cash flow**, and **personal tax benefits** (how investing in real estate saves you tax dollars over renting.) We touched on some of these points earlier, but I'll talk about them here in more detail.

APPRECIATION

Simply defined, appreciation is when you purchase an item like a home and it goes up in value. For instance, if you purchase a home for $100,000 and in five years that same home is worth $125,000, your home has appreciated by $25,000.

The question I get in my real estate office from first-time homebuyers and investors is, "How do I guarantee appreciation?" Well, there is really no way to guarantee appreciation. However, you can make educated and informed choices that increase your chances of appreciation.

One way to help create appreciation is to look for undervalued property. Whether you are a first-time homebuyer or first-time investor, this advice can make you thousands in return. Take the real estate boom of the late 1990s and 2000s. Many investors were searching for homes that needed a little bit of repair in the hopes of flipping these homes for profit. Because the market was on an upward swing, they were able to enhance the home's value by cleaning and repairing it, therefore enabling them to command a higher price when they went to sell the home or refinance it.

What happens when you are trying to buy outside of a real estate boom? If you are, that doesn't mean you will not realize any appreciation on your property. Take the first example I gave of the two-family home in Boston. It was purchased for $7,000 and 40 years later it was worth over a half million dollars! Basic upkeep was all that was needed for this home to command this price, and it had weathered many real estate booms and busts and still gained value.

Do you have to wait 40 years to see profit on your home?

Absolutely not. Market conditions drive housing prices. If you purchase your home at a price that is above market value, it may take you a few years to start seeing a profit, but you will see a change in value. Unlike investing in stocks where a volatile market can spell disaster for a portfolio, real estate investments have a much lower risk and have the potential to realize appreciation even in a tough market.

CASH FLOW

I am a product of the rap and hip-hop generation. One of my favorite songs is a song by Wu-Tang Clan called "C.R.E.A.M." or CASH RULES EVERYTHING AROUND ME! Whether you like rap or not, you cannot disagree with their assertion: CASH or CASH FLOW rules everything. If your business, household, or personal finances are not cash flowing they are not doing well. The same theory applies for real estate investing.

Cash flow is the difference between the income that a property produces and the monthly expenses that the property has. For instance, if you have a two-family home with a $1,200 per month mortgage and pay $4500 per year for real estate taxes and insurance, your minimum monthly expenses for the property are $1,575.00. This means you will have to rent out both units (rental apartments are listed as units) for at least $790 each to break even each month. If rents in your area are going for $950 per month, you will have an excess of $325 each month in the form of cash flow. For every home you purchase that has cash flow, that's money in your pocket!

Cash flow is THE most important factor in real estate investing. We will talk more about investing in real estate in later chapters. However, I think it is important to let you know now that if you don't have cash flow you probably don't have an investment. There are many "investors" out there with "get rich quick schemes" that only want people to invest for appreciation. That is extremely dangerous. Remember: C.R.E.A.M!!

TAX BENEFITS

Uncle Sam always gets paid. You know that and he knows that. How do you pay him less? Purchase real estate. If you are reading this book and you have never purchased a home, you are currently giving the maximum amount of money in taxes to Uncle Sam. As you grow in income, your tax liability grows. To decrease that liability you have to look for itemized deductions. Now I am not a CPA, so always check with your tax professional for your specific case. However, I do know that you can deduct real estate expenses from your income so that the income you pay taxes on is less. Owning real estate affords the owner lucrative tax benefits not available to people who rent property. When you own a home, you can deduct the interest on your mortgage, local and state real estate taxes, and any upgrades the government allows such as replacing windows, adding new insulation, etc. A tax professional can give you more information about exactly what deductions are available to you, but these are the most common.

When you rent a home, you don't get any tax break. You pay your rent each month to your landlord and your landlord gets to write off the expenses of the property on his or her taxes. It doesn't seem fair if you're the one who's paying down his mortgage with your rent money, but that's the way the IRS tax laws work.

So it benefits you to own your own home and take these tax breaks yourself. For instance, if you pay $8,000 a year in interest payments on your mortgage and another $3,000 in taxes on your property, you have $11,000 to deduct off your federal taxes! Why is this important? Let's do a comparison.

Person A/Renter/Single
Income:	**$45,000 per year**
Rent:	**$1,000 per month**
Standard IRS Deduction:	$5,500
Total Deduction Allowed:	$5,500

Person B/Homeowner/Single

Income:	$45,000 per year
Mortgage Interest:	$8,000 per year
Property Taxes:	$3,000 per year
State Income Tax:	$1,350 per year
Car Excise Tax:	$145.00 per year
Total Deduction Allowed:	$12,495

From this illustration, you can see that Person B is allowed $6,995 more in deductions on his or her Federal Income Tax Return than Person A. How does that translate into money? Because both Person A and Person B are in the 15% tax bracket, it means that Person B will be saving $1,049 in taxes as 15% of $6,995 is $1,049. That's money in Person B's pocket that he or she can use to invest, put in the bank, or spend!

That's the homeowner's tax benefit at work. So, as you can see, there are many benefits to homeownership versus renting a home from a landlord. Let's recap here:

- Owning your own home can be a personal achievement that is satisfying.
- Owning your own home can be an investment that gains equity while you live in it.
- Owning your own home or other real estate can bring you cash flow each month.
- Owning your own home can give you tax savings that renting can't give you.

Investors know that to build wealth quickly, you need to invest in real estate. Real estate, despite the ups and downs of the market, continues to be the best place for a person to invest his or her money and realize real gains.

In the coming chapters, I'll explain step by step what it takes for you to purchase your first home and then to continue to purchase investment homes to build wealth.

3

Yes! You Can Finance Your 40 Acres
"There is NO Romance without Finance!"
My Grandmother

That's right! There IS no romance without finance. You have heard that before and I know you may think it's not true, but I am here to tell you that you can have everything you need on a date but if your money is funny you are going to have a problem. I have changed that axiom for real estate purposes. There is NO HOUSE without Finance. You must have your financing in order BEFORE you start the home-buying process.

One of the things that amazes me on a daily basis is the number of calls we get at my real estate company from people who want to go see a home but have not taken the time to get pre-approved for a mortgage. Purchasing real estate is not like buying a car. Most people, when they shop for a car, look for the car first and then look for the financing. A car is personal property and typically can be financed easily even with credit or employment issues. A home purchase is typically going to be the largest financial transaction of your life. You have to take the time to get pre-approved so that you know your options and what programs are available to you.

On a daily basis, I see Black folks who are intimidated by the mortgage process. Let's get this out of the way: as Jamie Foxx used to say as Wanda, "Don't be SCARED!" You must know where you are to know where you are going! That's in everything in life, including buying a home. In fact, I believe you should not even start looking until you have sat down with a mortgage professional. The money portion of a real estate transaction can make or break whether that transaction is good for you or not.

I see so many of us wait until it's too late and then try to get financed. They then become disappointed because either they don't qualify at all or they qualify for a mortgage that is not a good option for them at the time. By the time they get this news, however, they have fallen in love with the house and are willing to do anything to purchase it. That's how most people end up in foreclosure. They didn't take prudent steps in the beginning to find out where they truly stood financially. Don't make that mistake. Take your time. Don't be in a hurry. If the house you are looking at goes to someone else, there are always others.

Let's take a look at the numbers so you can see how times are changing for all African-Americans. United States Census figures show that in 1993, 42.6% of all African-Americans owned their own home. In 2004 that number jumped to 49.5%. It is still a far cry, however, from the 75.7% of all white Americans who own their own home.

GENERATIONAL WEALTH

Why are these numbers important? One of the legacies of being enslaved as a people, in my opinion, is the inability to build and create generational wealth. What is generational wealth? It is creating wealth and passing that wealth on from generation to generation. How are our white brothers and sisters able to have a financial leg up in each successive generation? Their grandparents, parents, aunts, and uncles will them a financial foundation that puts them ahead. In the work I do every day as a real estate broker and mortgage broker, I can't tell you the number of times my white clients have come and been able to either pay cash or put more than 20% down on a home because of money they were willed from their elders. In order for Black folks to unravel the bonds of this legacy, we must create generational wealth. To do this, we must own our homes and own investment properties! The wealth that this creates can be passed on to our children and our children's children. So don't be scared to start the process by filling out a simple mortgage application! At no other time in history has it been easier for Black folks to own homes. Now let's get educated!

EDUCATION IS THE KEY!

The United States Census study in 2004 cites the reason for the increase in African-American homeownership as being education and availability of mortgage programs such as Fannie Mae to the African-American population. While programs such as Fannie Mae always existed, many African-Americans didn't know that such loans were available to them or even if they qualified. Since the inception of the education program in 1993, the number of Fannie Mae loans given to African-Americans rose a staggering 323%.

MORTGAGE SCAMS

The government also warned that while education was a main factor in increasing the number of African-American home loans, education about shady loans was also important.

I have to take time out to address mortgage scams and Black folks. Unfortunately, there are many lenders who seek out minority groups and offer unfair terms that make it harder for minorities to not only buy a home, but keep the home once they've purchased it. Before we go into the different types of financing, let's talk about how to spot a crook. I have seen it time and time again--honest people who get caught up with dishonest "professionals." I know this has been said before but remember these words, "If it sounds too good to be true, then it is!" Here are a few things to look for and ask for when looking and applying for a mortgage. If you don't get these things answered, you are putting yourself at risk:

- <u>Always ask to see a Good Faith Estimate!</u> Why? The Good Faith Estimate is supposed to show you what fees you are being charged by the mortgage company. A federal law mandates that you must be given a Good Faith Estimate within three days of application.

  Most people that call me who have been scammed were never given a Good Faith Estimate. They tell me of stories where the loan officer just told them they would need $1,000 or no money and they believed them. They then go to close on their house and all of a sudden, they need five or ten times more than they were told. Always get a Good Faith Estimate! Even if the loan officer is not sure what program you are approved for at that time, he or she can give you some estimate of your cost.

- <u>Typical up front fees to apply for a mortgage should not be more than $400 to $500 dollars.</u> This fee should include the cost to do your appraisal. I have had many clients call and tell me that they gave $5,000 or $10,000 dollars for a guaranteed approval. They were also told that they wouldn't need any additional money. If you are paying more than $400, you should be very leery of the person that you are talking with.

- Straw Buyer Scam: Here is how this works — someone contacts you saying they have a great investment plan for you. If you purchase a particular investment property, you will not only get a great deal on the property but you will also get THOUSANDS of dollars back at closing. Let's say $10,000. But wait, there's more. The person will typically tell you that they already have a renter ready to rent the home and cover your new mortgage. They are just looking for the right investor.

    If you are approached with this opportunity, RUN FAST in the opposite direction. There are so many laws being broken in this transaction that I would have to write another book to cover them all. Just to give you a few: a buyer is typically not allowed to receive "cash back" at closing. If the lender knew about it, the loan would be invalidated. In addition, these deals are typically done with fraudulent appraisals, closing companies, and loan officers. In recent years, the FBI has actually set up special task forces just to combat these problems. So remember, if it sounds too good to be true it typically is.

WHERE DO I GET FINANCING FOR MY 40 ACRES?

Let's talk about different types of financing and how to choose which type is best for you before you search for a home. You can obtain financing from two different sources: a mortgage banker or a mortgage broker.

Mortgage Banker

When a person wants to buy a house and needs financing, the first thing that comes to mind is to go down to their local bank and apply for a loan. A mortgage banker is a financial institution that, simply said, lends their own money. You see them on a daily basis; Bank of America, Countrywide, and Washington Mutual are all large mortgage banks. They take money they have in their deposits and make mortgage loans with them. A mortgage banker manages your loan from start to finish and has the money on hand to loan you. They will take you from the prequalification process all the way through the closing of a loan within the mortgage bank; you have loan officers, who can also be called mortgage consultants or loan consultants. Your loan officer knows everything about your loan and the status of it at any given time throughout the process, and can also recommend one type of loan over another for your particular needs.

When you get financing through a bank, you are working with an employee of that bank until the loan is completed. One constraint of working with a mortgage bank is they only have access to THEIR mortgage programs. Mortgage banks typically have quite a few programs. However, they don't have every program to fit every borrower's situation. That's typically where mortgage brokers come into play.

Mortgage Broker

A mortgage broker is simply that, a broker. Instead of working at one bank, they work with dozens, if not hundreds, of banks to obtain loans for their clients. They are an agent for the loan. They are compensated by brokering their clients' loans to a particular mortgage bank.

I am both a mortgage banker and mortgage broker. I have clients ask me all the time, why should they use mortgage brokers? The answer is really flexibility. Because a mortgage broker is not constrained by one set of mortgage products, they can provide a multiplicity of mortgage programs to their clients. With that flexibility, they can typically find better deals than mortgage banks, in my opinion.

Finally, here is what you can do to protect yourself:

- Ask questions of the loan officer. This is what he

or she gets paid for! Make sure you pay attention
to the answers and are comfortable with all
aspects of the loan and the terms.

- Shop around. Don't just go with the first lender
  you see in the phone book. My advice is to ask the
  realtor you are working with. Typically, they
  have lending relationships they trust. Remember,
  as a real estate professional, your realtor does not
  get paid until you close on a home. Because of
  that, they have developed relationships with
  lenders that they know are good and can take care
  of their clients. Of course, only ask your realtor if
  YOU trust him or her.

- Do your research on lending BEFORE you fall in
  love with a home. I can see that you are doing
  that by reading this book. However, don't let
  your research stop here. Pick up a copy of *Home
  Buying for Dummies* and books like that. I love to
  work with educated clients and I am sure there are
  other professionals out there who feel the same.

- Know the fees associated with getting the loan.
  Some lenders charge outrageous fees to give you a
  ¼ point lower on your mortgage. Remember,
  ALWAYS get a copy of the Good Faith Estimate

before you decide which lender to use.

So you have found your mortgage company. Now let's talk about the 1,000-pound gorilla in the room… CREDIT.

4

Putting Your Credit in Order
Don't Be Scared!!!" – Jamie Fox as Wanda

The definition of FEAR is FALSE EVIDENCE
APPEARING REAL. In my 10 years of practicing real estate, the
number one factor that has kept Black folks from even seeking
the opportunity for homeownership is FEAR. We are simply
scared of the process. What does that fear rise out of? We are
SCARED to see our credit reports! There are a couple of reasons
for this, I have found:

1. <u>You have been irresponsible with your credit and you
   don't want anyone to see your dirty little secrets.</u> You
   are embarrassed because credit is a very personal thing. I
   get that. However, there is no way you can know where
   you're going if you cannot determine where you are. All
   of us, especially when we were young, have had credit
   issues here and there. Even if that's not the case for you
   and you have just been, as my mom would say, "triflin',"
   it's O.K. As she would also say, you are not the first nor
   the last to do so. The most important thing now would

be to change your ways so that you can put yourself in a position to purchase your home.

Do lenders care about your past credit issues? Yes. However, I can tell you a number of stories where my clients have done the work that I will describe in this chapter and come back to us with credit scores that allow them to purchase a home. So it's O.K. to let someone in to see your closet. That's the only way you're going to get it cleaned!

2. <u>Most of us have NO IDEA what's on our credit report.</u> I have had clients with GREAT credit tell me they have no clue as to their score and some even think they have "bad" credit. In addition to not knowing, some don't want to know. They feel that "what they don't know won't hurt them." That's crazy. It's kind of like a superstition. They are thinking, "If someone pulls my credit report then my secret will be revealed and I will have bad luck from here on out." Let me set the record straight: pulling your credit report only gives lenders the information they need to make an informed decision.

The example I like to use with my clients is this. Say your cousin and I came to you and asked to borrow $1,000. Of course, you know your cousin and probably have a good sense of his history of paying things.

However, other than reading this book, you don't know me from Adam. What other mechanism would you need to know whether you would want to lend me the money? Of course, you would want some references from other people who lent me money and how I paid them back, right? That's all a credit report is. It's a reference. If your references have said that you are paying them on time and in full, then you are O.K. If they are saying the opposite, then you may need to negotiate with your references and pay them off or get new references!

Lack of knowledge is like a tree without roots--it cannot grow! Knowledge in real estate comes by knowing where you are financially. That's what a credit report does. It gives the lender a fair assessment of where your current financial picture is. So don't be scared!

DEFINITION OF A CREDIT SCORE

The question I get all the time is, "What is a credit score and what does it mean?" My definition of a credit score is: <u>a statistical representation of what you will do in the future based on what you did in the past.</u> More specifically--based on what you did in the last six (6) months, what are the chances of you defaulting in the next six (6) months to a year? That's all it is.

The thinking is the higher your credit score the LESS likely you are to default (meaning not pay back) on a loan over the next six months. The reverse is also true. The lower your credit score the MORE likely you are to default on a loan in the future.

The number assigned is not arbitrary. FICO has a system for looking at the information in your credit file and coming up with this number. What they use is a report card. They run your information through this report card and out pops your credit score.

FACTORS THAT IMPACT YOUR CREDIT SCORE

Here are the factors that go into calculating your FICO score.

- **Payment history** – Each time you make a payment on a credit card, car loan, or other loan it shows up on your credit report. If a payment is made 30 days or more late, it is reported to the credit bureau and appears on the report. The credit report lists each month and number of times a payment is late.

  It also shows how recent the late payment was made. If a lender sees a few late payments three years ago and then everything paid on time since that date, they are likely to chalk that up to a bad situation. Lenders look closer at current data even though your credit history can go back for years!

Payment history encompasses 35% of the total FICO score; therefore, it is THE MOST IMPORTANT FACTOR that impacts your credit rating. Simply said, make sure you make your payments on your credit cards and loans on time.

- **Total amount owed on credit cards and loans** – Up to 30% of your credit score will consist of your total debt owed. A lender will consider the type of account, the total amount borrowed, and the amount paid off. If you have revolving credit, the lender will also look at your debt-to-owe ratio, which is the percent of available credit you have in comparison to your loan. The report cards that the credit reporting agencies use basically say that they don't want you to use more than 30% of your total available credit. Once you go above that number, your score actually starts to move downward. The closer you get to 100% utilization of your credit, the lower your score goes. What does this mean to you? Keep your balances on your credit cards low!

- **Credit history** – A lender will also look at your credit history and your lack of credit history. There are some people who do not like buying anything on credit and prefer to only purchase items if they have the cash on hand. While that is a smart move that will keep you from getting yourself into debt, it doesn't tell a lender if you are creditworthy should you borrow money. Since your credit history consists of 15% of your credit score, it is smarter to take out a credit card or loan and pay it back immediately so that you can show you are responsible and pay your debts.

- **New credit** – Ten percent of your score will consist of any new debt you've incurred in the last few months. Also, if you've been shopping around for loans for a car to see if you can get the best price, this will show up on your credit score. However, lenders are generally aware that consumers want to shop around and get the best deal, so when they see multiple requests for credit information and everything else checks out on the report, they're more likely to overlook it.

    TIP: You can shop for a mortgage. As long as you do it over a 30-day period, the credit reporting agencies will only hit you with one inquiry. However, if you are shopping for something like a car, each time someone pulls your credit it is counted as an inquiry.

Although inquiries only count for 10% of your score, it is important to keep them as low as possible.

- **Overall mix of credit** – When looking at your credit report, a lender will want to see more than just one type of credit that you've handled. For instance, if you've only had department store charge cards, that doesn't tell the lender if you'll be able to handle a new car loan. But if the lender looks at your report and sees that you've had a successful car loan that is paid off, a credit card or two, and perhaps a personal or student loan that has not gone in default, it shows that you can manage your credit.

The credit bureaus that calculate your credit score are required by law to give you a copy of your credit report at least once per year so that you can check through it and make sure it is accurate. Many times, there are mix-ups in a particular credit item. When you do find an error and report it to the credit bureau, the credit bureau is required to fix the error immediately and send you a revised report.

There are three major credit bureaus who give out credit reports. They are Experian, Trans Union, and Equifax. It's best to get a free copy of your credit report from all three credit bureaus, as information could be different on each of them and you'll want to compare to make sure they are all accurate. You can obtain a copy of your free credit report at www.annualcreditreport.com.

I HAVE MY CREDIT REPORT. NOW WHAT?

Okay, you have your credit report. What do you do next? The first thing you need to do is make sure that all the debt that shows on your credit report is really yours. It is amazing how many times someone else's credit card bill or loan payment will appear on a report erroneously. For instance, if your mother or father has the same name as you, you may see one or two items appear on your report that actually belong to them, especially if you've lived at the same address recently.

If this is the case and you find something that shouldn't be on your credit report, write the credit bureau and detail the information supporting this error asking them to remove the error immediately. It's one thing to have your own debt on a report. It's quite another if someone else's debt is affecting your ability to purchase a home. Once you've written the credit bureaus, wait 30 days and then call for another free credit report to make sure the error has been fixed.

LATE PAYMENTS AND COLLECTIONS

If you have made several late payments on your debt, it will appear on your credit report listing the number of days late as over 30 or over 60, etc. Each month you were delinquent with a payment will show on your report.

If any past debt has gone into collection, it will show on the report as well. Even if you've paid off the debt, the late payments and collection will be listed. While you've put yourself in a better position by paying off your debt, a new lender will look at how long ago that payoff was made and how your current payments have been to determine your creditworthiness.

Do not allow your debt to go into collection if you can help it. Most debt collectors are willing to work with you if you are honest and make a concerted effort to pay your balance.

REPAIRING YOUR CREDIT SCORE

Despite what you might think, you do have some control over your credit score and how to change it. The first step in repairing your credit score is getting a copy of your credit report, as stated earlier. The first thing you need to do is go through the report and contact the credit bureaus about any errors that are on the report. Then the real negotiations start.

If you have some credit cards that have high balances,

your goal is to pay down those balances. It may or may not be feasible to pay a credit card with a $5,000 balance off all in one shot, so make a plan to pay off your credit card over a period of a year or two. But before you can do that, you need to know how much money you can realistically put toward your debt. Here is what you will need to do:

- List all your fixed debt on a piece of paper. These are debts like your telephone and electrical bill, rent, food bill, etc. Total up all your fixed debt and add extra on for months when the electric bill might fluctuate a little.

- Add up all your revolving debt. Revolving debt would be your major and store credit cards. Put down the balance of each of them as well as the minimum payment and the interest rate you are currently being charged. Some credit card interest rates fluctuate, so taking an average is okay. Add up the minimum payments to get a minimum amount you must pay each month on your cards.

- Get out your calculator!

The easiest way to calculate the time it will take to pay your debt is by using a payment calculator that will take into consideration your interest rate and your balance. Simply taking the balance and dividing it by a payment amount you can afford doesn't work because interest on your debt will be added to the balance each month.

There are many payment calculators online that you can use to figure out how long it will take to pay off your debt. Bankrate.com has a payment calculator for just about any type of loan. If you have Internet access or can get to a library with computer and Internet access, I would start there first.

Gather up all your information and enter the totals into the payment calculator to give you a rough estimate of how long it will take you to pay off your debt if you DO NOT USE THAT CREDIT CARD AGAIN. This is very important. If you continue to use your revolving credit lines, your balance will never go down and you won't pay off your debt.

One other thing to note about making minimum payments is that they are designed to be beneficial for the lender, not the consumer. By paying the minimum payment, you are only putting a small amount of money on the principal of the loan. The rest is interest. So if you've only been paying the minimum balance on your credit cards, you'll need to start paying a bit more to get your balance down. This is why if you continue to use your credit card, your balance never goes down. You just continue to pay interest until you've maxed out your credit card.

Look at all your credit cards and put them in order of the highest interest rate to the lowest interest rate, and then put them in order of the highest balance to the lowest balance. Next, start with the credit card that has the highest interest rate. You want to start paying down the highest interest rate first because that one is the money hog. The longer you continue to pay a low amount on this credit card, the more interest will accumulate and the longer it will take for you to pay it off.

Let's take two different credit cards as an example. Say you have one credit card with a $1,500 balance and a 17% interest rate that has a minimum payment of $30 per month. Let's say you have another credit card with a $3,000 balance and a 30% interest rate that has a minimum payment of $80 per month. Yes, there are credit cards that charge as much as 30% if you've been delinquent on your bills in the past.

It may seem like it makes sense to pay off the lower balance first because it's easier to pay that one off than the higher balance. But it is actually better to pay off the credit card with the highest interest rate first unless the balance on the other credit cards is so low that you can pay them off within a month or two. You don't want to extend the months you'll be accruing high interest rates longer than you have to.

Taking the example above, the total minimum payments for the two credit cards is $110. To pay those credit cards off you'll want to increase the amount that you are paying by at least double or $220. Continue to pay the minimum amount on the lower interest rate card and use the additional $110 to add to your monthly payment of $80 on the higher interest rate card for a total of $190 a month. Instead of paying off the higher interest rate card in 109 months or just over nine years, you'll be able to pay off that credit card in 22 months or just under two years. This saves you $6,960 over the course of those years that would have all been interest if you didn't pay it off quickly.

Once you've paid off the first card, put the $190 you are paying on that card towards the second card. You have now reduced your debt seven years earlier than you would have if you'd only paid the minimum payment.

This strategy works even if you don't have a big lump sum of money at your disposal to pay down your debt. However, if you do have some money put aside that can be used towards paying off debts, you may want to try a different strategy.

SETTLE/NEGOTIATE

Sometimes it makes sense to pay off your credit card in one lump sum. Never pay off your debt without first calling the credit card company to try to negotiate a lower payoff figure. For instance, if you have $5,000 left on a credit card to pay it off but only have $4,000 in funds to put towards that credit card, see if you can negotiate a payout figure of $4,000 and have the credit card company "forgive" the other $1,000.

Not every credit card company will be willing to do this, but some will. The money you save is money you can put towards purchasing your home. NOTE: Please check with your tax advisor when you do this as some creditors report the loss as income to you. You don't want to end up with a surprise IRS tax bill.

5

Determining How Much House You Can Afford

"You got to fake it 'til you make it"
Unknown

That quote has gotten more Black folk in financial trouble than anything in history. Our people believe for some reason that what we have and how it looks determines not only our success but also what others think of us. I see it all the time in my real estate office. A client walks in that only can afford say a $150,000 house. However, in their mind they have to "fake it 'til they make it" and want to purchase something way bigger than that, say a $250,000 home. Why? Because, in their mind, what they can afford is not something they would be seen in or they see it as something beneath them. We see it every day on television shows like MTV Cribs where wealth is flaunted in front of us and made to seem like it's easily obtainable. What those shows don't show us is that many of those homes are either leased or the celebrity that owns the home has often taken on too much debt as well. So I would like to change the saying from "Fake it til you make it" to "Be real 'til you make it and then you can flaunt it".

Do you know what "House Poor" is? We use it in our business to describe someone who has a large house or house note but no furniture and/or can't afford anything else but the house note. That's a horrible situation to put yourself in. You do not want to be House Poor. Therefore, this chapter is dedicated to helping you determine how much house you can really afford.

In terms of purchasing a home, it is fun to drive through the city or town you live in and dream of living in one of those big, beautiful homes you see. Unfortunately, there are many of us unlike my description above who, despite their eligibility to afford these homes, think it isn't possible to ever achieve that dream.

That's a sad fact. No one should be denied homeownership and no one should ever be made to feel that they can't afford a home. By simply learning what it takes to become eligible to purchase a house, you will begin to think differently about those big, beautiful homes you drive by. Instead of wishing you could purchase that home with the front porch and big back yard, you'll be envisioning yourself living there.

Let's get down to brass tacks and talk about how much house you *really* can afford. You may be surprised at what you learn.

YOUR MORTGAGE PAYMENT

Let's start with your mortgage payment. When a lender looks at how much a person can afford for housing, they include several things to make up the total monthly payment and those things depend on what type of mortgage you get and how much money you have to put down on the house at the time of purchase. Your total monthly payment will include your principal, interest, and escrow.

Escrow is made up of extra expenses that a lender will add to the payment each month to make sure things like taxes and insurance on the house are paid in a timely manner. For instance, if you did not have at least 20% to use as a down payment on your house you may be subject to private mortgage insurance or PMI. This PMI helps insure the loan to make sure that if you default on your loan the bank will not lose money if they need to sell the home at a reduced rate.

Another fee that will be used as part of escrow is your homeowners insurance. The bank wants to make sure that in case something catastrophic happens to the house, any repairs that need to be made are covered. It not only insures you in case of damage, it helps insure the bank, so the bank will want to make sure that your insurance policy is current by making those payments.

The house or property taxes that you pay to the town or city you live in may also be included in your escrow amount. Most likely the bank will pay them on a yearly basis. If your total yearly taxes are $3,000, the bank will pay this amount at the end of the year for you to make sure the property taxes are up-to-date.

Some people don't like to have the bank hold their money. They'd rather pay for items such as house insurance and taxes themselves. However, unless you put a 20% down payment on the value of your home, the bank will generally insist on taking care of these items in escrow.

Even people who choose to put a 20% down payment on their home will choose to have the bank take care of their property taxes and homeowners insurance in escrow. It is sometimes easier to make that one payment per month than to hold money aside and make a lump sum payment.

INCOME

Generally, a lender will want to keep your payments on your new home to between 28 and 36% of your total gross income. There are some lenders who will go as high as 55%, but

I caution you not to overextend yourself by using those numbers unless your income clearly can handle debt that high. Pay close attention here--we are talking about GROSS income not NET Income. Gross Income is your income before payroll taxes are taken out. Many of my clients assume that when we talk about income we mean what their "take home pay" is. I understand that; we all tend to think of our finances in terms of what we bring home. In fact, I would encourage you to think of that when you are being qualified for a mortgage. Even though we as mortgage professionals may determine your affordability based on your gross, you need to think about what you actually take home. By using this method, you are assured that you don't OVERbuy a home that you truly cannot afford.

The income that you use to qualify for a mortgage can come from many different sources. For instance, if you work a day job and make a certain amount each week you will include that as part of your income as well as any part-time work you do as long as you have had the part-time job for at least two years. If you receive child support or alimony that income can be included as well towards your total income to qualify for a loan.

There are other sources of income that people can use to help them qualify for a loan. If you own any stocks that pay dividends on a regular basis, the dividends from those stocks can be used as income as long as you have a record of a consistent contribution to your monthly gross income for at least two years.

If you're married, you can choose to use your spouse's income or try to qualify on your own. But to give you the best chance of obtaining the mortgage and the terms that you want and that are more favorable for you, I recommend you use as many sources of income as you can to help you qualify for your loan.

Remember, just because you qualify for a high mortgage doesn't mean you need to take out a mortgage for the full amount. Each person has a different comfort level when it comes to debt. Whereas one couple may decide that they want to buy the biggest home that their money can buy, another couple might decide that they want to be able to afford their house based on just one of their incomes. Even if you are in the latter situation, however, it is still best to use both incomes to help you qualify for the loan.

EXAMPLES

Spouse #1 earns $45,000 per year at one job and an additional $10,000 per year working a second job. This means the total gross income for spouse number one is $55,000.

Spouse #2 earns $20,000 per year working a day job and

receives $10,000 annually for child support for children from a first marriage. The total amount that spouse #2 can list as gross income on a mortgage application is $30,000 per year.

$55,000 + $30,000 = $85,000 gross income per year

When applying for a mortgage this couple can list their total gross income as $85,000 per year and base this figure against what they can afford to purchase. However, the final number can change based on how much money the couple has to use as a down payment. Let's look at how this figure could play out.

Based on $85,000 gross income per year, this couple has a gross income of $7,083 per month. Using the 28% calculation, they can afford a payment for housing of $1983 per month. This doesn't mean that they can afford a mortgage payment of $1,983 per month. It means that the total amount they pay, which includes the principal on the mortgage, the interest on the mortgage, and any amount in escrow cannot exceed $1,983 per month.

For the sake of argument, let's say that the annual property taxes on a home at which this couple is looking are $3,000 per year. Their yearly property insurance rate is $800 per year. And since they did not have at least 20% to put down as a deposit, they also have a monthly PMI of $71 per month. This means that their monthly escrow amount would be $387. Since they qualify for a payment of $1,983 per month, we can deduct the escrow of $387 and are left with $1,596 per month that can be used for principal and interest payments.

Now this number has a lot of power, as does the interest rate that this couple is able to obtain based on their credit. This is why having the best credit you can have is so important. The better your credit rating, the lower the interest rate you will be able to qualify for.

To continue our example, we'll use a fixed interest rate of 6.5% amortized over a period of 30 years. This means that the total payments for the entire loan will be spread out over the course of 30 years and the mortgage payment will remain the same because it is a fixed loan. Using this calculation, this couple can afford a mortgage of $252,000.

If the couple's credit is not the best, they may still qualify for a mortgage with a higher interest rate. If they are able to obtain an interest rate of 8% for their mortgage, they would then be able to afford a mortgage of $217,000. That's a difference of $35,000!

Like I said earlier, lenders like to keep mortgage payments between 28 and 36%, although some will go higher. Let's look at another example using a monthly payment using the 36% debt ratio.

With a monthly gross income of $7,083, this couple

would be able to afford a monthly housing payment of $2,550 per month. Using the same escrow amount of $387 per month and a 6.5% fixed rate mortgage for 30 years, this couple can afford a mortgage of $341,000.

This means that using the 36% debt ratio for housing instead of the 28% debt ratio for housing, this couple can afford a home that is $90,000 more expensive. Again, not everyone will feel comfortable pushing the limits of what they can afford. However, if your income and the amount of debt that you currently have can support you making the payment comfortably there is no reason why you can't purchase the best house your money can buy.

THE ONE PERCENT (1%) RULE

The information above was very detailed and will be extremely helpful in helping you determine how much house you can afford. But let's say that you are out looking for a home and you don't have your calculator with you, but you want to determine how much a particular house would be on a monthly basis. Here is a great rule of thumb you can use until you meet with your mortgage advisor. Just take one percent (1%) of the sales price of the house and that will give you a good approximation of how much your monthly payment will be with Principle, Interest, Taxes and Insurance (PITI). Let's look at an example. You see a home that is priced at $150,000. Approximately how much would your monthly payment be? One percent of $150,000 equals $1,500 per month. Now this rule of thumb makes a couple of assumptions:

- It assumes you are putting at least a 5% down payment on the purchase of the home. If you are not, then the rule changes to One Percent plus $100 (1% + $100) to factor in a higher financed amount

- This rule assumes an interest rate between 6.5% and 7%. If your rate is going to be higher then you may need to add $30 to $40 dollars to the One Percent Amount

YOUR TOTAL DEBT

In the prior chapter I talked about cleaning up your credit report and getting rid of your debt. There are clearly certain types of debt that you need to clean up completely before you try to get a mortgage so that your application looks more favorable to the lender. However, there are some debts that are harder to get rid of but are taken into consideration when you apply for a mortgage.

If you have a car loan, the lender will want to know how much your monthly payment is, what your car is worth, and how much you have left to pay on your loan. The lender will know your credit history with the bank that handles your car loan, so you want to make sure that you're making your payments on time every month. Other debt that you may have is a student loan. Again, you want to make your payments on time and, if it all possible, you want to pay this debt off quickly to make your application look as appealing as possible to the lender.

How much debt is too much debt? A mortgage lender will not want to see any debt at all, but if you do have some it cannot be more than 38% of your total gross income. This percentage includes your monthly mortgage and escrow. For someone who is using the 28% debt ratio to figure out a monthly housing payment, this would leave 10% of your monthly gross income available for debt or $708 per month. This $708 per month can be used to pay for student loans or car payments. But if the amount you pay is higher than $708 per month, you need to pay this debt down before you purchase your home.

If the couple above was using the 36% debt ratio it would leave them very little wiggle room. They would only have $142 per month available to use for other debt.

OTHER DEBT THE LENDER WILL NOT CONSIDER

There are other factors that people need to pay attention to on a monthly basis that your lender will not care about. For instance, your lender will not ask you how much your car insurance is even if you own a fancy sports car and pay a high monthly car insurance premium. Your lender will also not care how much you're paying in daycare expenses. But these figures need to be taken into consideration when you're factoring in how much you feel comfortable paying each month for a mortgage.

For instance, you may not have any debt outside of your monthly mortgage payment and escrow, but you may be paying $1,000 per month in childcare expenses. In a case like this, even though you would qualify using the 36% debt ratio, you may want to consider using the 28% debt ratio, at least until you no longer have that $1,000 childcare expense every month. Many couples with young children get themselves in trouble if they don't factor in their total debt.

Remember, you can always buy a smaller house now, pay down the mortgage for a few years and build equity, and then buy a larger house later on when you no longer have high monthly childcare bills.

DOWN PAYMENT

When you purchase a home the lender will want to know how much money you are putting down as a deposit. While there are some mortgage programs that require little or no money down, lenders like to see that you are investing in your home. The higher the down payment by the homeowner, the lower the risk to the lender because if you default on your mortgage the lender has less money to recoup.

Your down payment can come from many different sources. If you have steadily been saving for a down payment on a house, make sure you keep copies of your bank statements that show your deposits. This shows the lender that you're responsible and are able to put aside a certain amount of money every month.

You can also borrow the money against a 401(k) program or insurance policy that you own. Many whole life insurance policies have cash values and the owners of these policies are able to take loans against that money.

If a family member gives you a chunk of money as a gift, you can use that as a down payment as well. Lenders generally do not like to see all of the money for the deposit gifted to the homeowner, as it does not show that the homeowner is able to save and be consistent with making payments. However, a money gift from a family member can help reduce the amount of mortgage you need to pay, so don't overlook that as a source of money for a down payment.

CLOSING COSTS

You have your down payment, you have all your papers in order and ready to give your lender, and suddenly someone mentions the words **closing costs**. Closing costs are the fees associated with taking out a mortgage with the lender. These fees can range anywhere from a few hundred dollars to several thousand dollars. Depending on the type of mortgage you get and the lender you choose, closing costs vary widely, so you need to take this into consideration when you're looking for a lender.

Closing costs consist of a mortgage application fee, appraisal fee on the property, any filing fees for the title, title search fees, points that you pay to the lender for taking out the loan, and attorney costs both for the bank and for yourself. There may also be a prorated payment included as part of the closing costs. This prorated payment is usually added in when the mortgage is taken out in the middle of the month. It covers the prorated amount of your mortgage payment for that month. If you close on your loan at the end of the month, it may even include the mortgage payment for the next month, giving you almost two months before you have to make your first payment.

Some lenders allow the homeowner to finance all or part of their closing costs in with their mortgage. Some people do not want to finance fees over the course of 30 years; however, it may be beneficial to do this if you do not have enough cash on hand to pay your closing costs up front.

All these amounts will be taken into consideration when you apply for a mortgage on the home. Decreasing your monthly debt goes a long way towards making your application favorable to a lender. Keeping good records of the amount of money you're saving and the sources you're getting your deposit amount from will also make it easier for you to qualify for a mortgage that suits your needs. Use the following table to help you figure out how much mortgage you can afford.

Mortgage Affordability Worksheet

Monthly Income	**Monthly Amt.**
Wages and Salary (include overtime and bonuses)	$_____
Investment income	$_____
Child Support and Alimony	$_____
Total Monthly Income	$_____
Total Monthly Debt	
Credit card payments	$_____
Student loans	$_____
Car payments	$_____
Total Monthly Debt outside of housing payment	$_____

38% of $_____ (total monthly income)   A $_____
28% of $_____ (total monthly income   B $_____
36% of $_____ (total monthly income)   C $_____
A $_____minus $_____(total monthly debt) D $_____

6

Types of Financing Available
"Life is like a box of chocolates--you never know what you gonna get."
Forrest Gump

I do believe what Forrest Gump says. Life is like a box of chocolates but buying a home is not. You DO know what you are going to get because you have choices. I want my people to know that you do not have to be forced into a particular mortgage product. Many African-Americans now find themselves in dire financial situations because they were not aware of the different mortgage products available to them. That's where this book comes into play. Contrary to what some people believe, you don't need a degree in finance to understand mortgage financing. But to make sure that you are getting the right mortgage that fits your needs you do need to have a little bit of understanding about which mortgages are available to you.

For most people, a home is the biggest purchase they will make in their lifetime. It is easy to fall victim to all the different scams from unscrupulous mortgage professionals if you do not have the basics of mortgage financing behind you.

Whether this is your first home or the tenth home that you've purchased, you need to keep abreast of things like current interest rates, adjustable versus fixed rates, the benefits of 15- and 30-year mortgages and when any of these options is right for you.

FIXED-RATE MORTGAGES

A fixed-rate mortgage is one where the payments for the mortgage remain the same for the life of the loan. When rates are low like they are now, it is beneficial to get a fixed-rate mortgage because you won't have to worry about changes in the economy affecting interest rates and making your payments increase.

For those who want the comfort of knowing exactly what they will be paying each month, a fixed-rate mortgage is the only way to go. You need to look at your comfort level and whether or not you expect that your income will increase over time enough to keep up with any fluctuations in the market.

Also, if you plan on purchasing a home for the long haul and living in it for a long period of time, you may do better with a fixed-rate mortgage as you will not have to deal with fluctuations in the market over a period of up to 30 years.

Economic changes are a given, and if you don't want to ride the wave of economic change, a fixed-rate mortgage is your best bet.

ADJUSTABLE-RATE MORTGAGES

An adjustable-rate mortgage is one where the interest rate is generally lower and is tied either every year or every few years to the prime rate. If the prime rate for lending goes up, your adjustable-rate mortgage will adjust up as well, costing you more money each month for your mortgage.

When you choose an adjustable-rate mortgage, the lender will stipulate how often an adjustment can be made so that you can anticipate to some degree whether or not your mortgage will stay the same or increase. Adjustable-rate mortgages can adjust anywhere from every six months to every two years.

Also, there is a cap on how many points your adjustable rate can change. For instance, if you currently have an adjustable-rate mortgage, say at 6% for two years, and the prime rate suddenly shoots up, the lender can only increase the adjustable rate the maximum number of points stipulated in the mortgage note.

Adjustable-rate mortgages are good for people who do not expect to be in the home they're purchasing for a long period of time. The benefit is they get to have a lower interest rate for a short period of time, saving them interest each month on their loan, without having to worry about the rate adjusting to a level that is too high for them to afford.

INTEREST-ONLY MORTGAGES

In the past few years there have been an increasing number of what are known as interest-only mortgages. On the outside, an interest-only mortgage sounds very attractive to a prospective homeowner. It offers you the ability to obtain a much higher mortgage with a lower payment. Interest-only loans have become so popular that many lenders have said that as many as 70% of all loans are now interest-only loans.

But there is danger in entering into an interest-only mortgage unless you plan on owning a home for an extremely short period of time or have a strategy for using this type of mortgage. For one thing, when you pay on an interest-only loan you are only paying interest and not paying down the principal on your loan. In order to pay off the loan the monthly mortgage payment will need to go up, and when it does it is usually at a much higher rate than that of an adjustable mortgage rate.

Many homeowners find the first few years of an interest-rate only mortgage beneficial to pay down debt or to save money. However, after a few years as the payment increases, the monthly payment may start to become unmanageable. If your income doesn't rise as fast as the increase in your interest-only mortgage payment, you may find it hard to keep up with your payments and could end up going into default on the loan when they become too overwhelming.

Interest-only mortgages are being blamed for the high number of foreclosures on the market today. While they are very attractive as a way to get into the home of your dreams, choosing this type of loan could end up turning into a nightmare. Proceed with caution if you are considering an interest-only loan.

DIFFERENT DOCUMENTATION TYPES OF A MORTGAGE LOAN

Full Documentation

Not only do the types of mortgages vary, the types of documentation that each lender requires also vary. A full-documentation mortgage or "full doc" mortgage is just that, one where the lender requires full documentation of all financial information. The borrower has to provide proof of everything that is written on the loan application.

If you work for an employer, you'll want to have several copies of your paycheck stubs, making sure you have the most recent to show the lender not only that you're still employed but how much you've made this year to date. If you work more than one job or your spouse works you'll want to have copies of those paycheck stubs as well.

Some lenders will also ask you for copies of your bank statements. As mentioned in the previous chapter, some lenders want to make sure the money that you are using to put down on your home is your own and that you can show that you saved for the money. It's okay to receive a gift for all or part of your down payment. But make sure you can prove that you also have money of your own to put down.

You will also need copies of your W-2 forms for the last two years. This shows the bank that you have steady income. And since you probably have copies of any IRA or retirement forms filed with your taxes, you'll need to make copies of these for the bank as well.

Stated Documentation

If you are self-employed, you won't have any paycheck stubs to show a lender. You will need to rely on your business records to prove your income and show a copy of your 1040 tax forms as proof of your income. For people who are self-employed, the paperwork involved in obtaining a mortgage can be daunting.

Because of this, some lenders allow for what is known as stated documentation. This type of mortgage is easier for people who either have income that fluctuates from month to month or for people who have a harder time proving to the lender how much income they earn.

Because this type of mortgage is considered a higher risk than full-documentation mortgages, many times the terms of the loan will not be as favorable as those for a full-documentation mortgage. The borrower ends up paying a higher interest rate, costing them more money over the life of the loan.

FHA/VA Mortgages

Federal Housing Administration or FHA mortgages are one of the most popular mortgages for first-time homebuyers, but you don't have to be a first-time homebuyer to qualify for one. Although they are similar to conventional mortgages, FHA mortgages are different. For one thing, the credit requirements for an FHA mortgage are more lenient than those for conventional mortgages. This gives a person with less-than-perfect credit a chance to qualify for a mortgage at a rate that is comparable to those of conventional loans.

FHA loans are insured by the government, which allows lenders the security of giving a higher risk borrower a loan. Not only are the interest rates competitive, the requirement for the amount of down payment is much lower than it is for a conventional mortgage. With an FHA loan you can purchase a home with as little as 3% down.

The downside of an FHA mortgage is having an added cost to your monthly payments in the way of private mortgage insurance or PMI. PMI is an insurance premium paid to the government to insure that in case you default on your loan the lender won't be out the money of the conventional 20% down payment.

On the plus side, you won't have to continue paying PMI for the life of your mortgage. As soon as the amount owed on the loan reaches 80% of the original value of the loan, you can apply to stop the private mortgage insurance.

Another plus to an FHA mortgage is that all of the down payment can be obtained either as a gift, through a grant, or through a down payment assistance program. This is a real benefit for people who want to own their own home but have difficulty saving enough money to cover a down payment and closing costs.

Veterans Administration or VA mortgages are similar to FHA mortgages in that the borrower does not need a large chunk of money to use for a down payment. However, not everyone can get a VA mortgage.

If you were in any branch of the military and were honorably discharged, you may qualify for a VA mortgage. VA mortgages go a little further than FHA mortgages because with a VA mortgage the borrower can qualify for a loan without any down payment at all. Also, the debt-to-income ratio is a little more lenient with a VA mortgage.

A VA mortgage program is a great way for people who have served time in the military to become homeowners. This program allows flexibility where some of the more conventional programs do not. Closing costs on the VA mortgage may be a little higher than those of a conventional mortgage. But given the benefits of being able to purchase a home with no money down, and also qualify for the loan if your credit is not the best or if your income level does not allow for a conventional loan, a VA mortgage is very appealing to many homebuyers.

Owner Financing

Banks and mortgage companies aren't the only lenders available to extend you a mortgage. Depending on the situation, the owner of the property that you're trying to purchase may agree to "take back" a mortgage for all or part of the price of the home. This strategy is wonderful for people who don't have a lot of money to put down or who can't qualify for any other loan due to credit limitations. Owner financing is just that: the owner becomes the lender and instead of you paying your monthly mortgage to a bank or mortgage company, you pay it to the original owners of the house.

You might be asking yourself why a person would want to take back a mortgage. Why not just get all the money up front? Well, some people sell a home with the intention of taking the profit they make from the home and putting it in the bank. If the current interest rate is 3% for a savings account and the current interest rate to get a mortgage with a bank is 7%, the owner makes a better profit by extending a loan for a higher interest rate than simply putting the money in the bank.

The restrictions for owner financing are many times more lenient than that of conventional financing. But don't count on the owner not doing a credit check or income verification. Like a bank, the owner who extends a mortgage to a buyer will want to make sure that the buyer can pay back the loan in a timely manner.

While not common, some owners will finance a home for 100% of the purchase price over a 30-year period. More likely though, the owner will finance a portion of the mortgage, say 20%, and have that amortized over a period of 30 years but with a balloon payment for the balance due after five or ten years. This means that the buyer has the benefit of paying a lower amount for their loan while the equity in their home increases.

After five or ten years, when the balance is due, the buyer can then refinance their home to pay off the balance of the owner financing or pay it off with funds they have on hand.

Lease Purchase/Lease Option

Yet another way to purchase a home is through a lease/purchase or a lease/option. A lease/purchase is popular if for some reason the home has been on the market for a long period of time and the owner is worried that it will not sell. It doesn't mean there's anything wrong with the home. It could simply mean that the market is glutted with homes for sale.

In a lease/purchase, the buyer will agree to lease the property for a certain period of time with the stipulation that at the end of the lease they will purchase the home. Usually there is an agreed-upon time to lease the property of approximately one or two years so the owner does not have to wait a long time for the purchase to go through. This type of arrangement is beneficial to the owner in that they know that when entering into this type of arrangement their house will be sold.

A lease/option is similar to a lease/purchase but with one difference. In a lease/option, the buyer leases the property and has the option during the leasing period to decide whether or not they want to purchase the home.

This type of arrangement, while still popular, has more

risk to the seller in that there is no guarantee that the person leasing the property will end up purchasing the home at the end of the lease. If the home does not end up being sold, the seller needs to start all over again to find a new buyer.

This is just another beneficial way that a person with less than perfect credit or not much money to put down can become a homeowner without having to get a mortgage the conventional way. Also, the buyer can negotiate with the seller that part of the money paid each month towards the lease can be used as a down payment at the time the house is purchased. This gives the buyer a chance to live in the home for a while and save money for the purchase.

Grants/First-Time Homebuyer Programs

Federal, State, and non-profit organizations have programs available for first-time homebuyers and for low-income buyers. These programs are extremely worthwhile to help the first-time homebuyer become a homeowner.

One of the best ways to find these programs is by visiting the Housing and Urban Development, or HUD, website at http://www.hud.gov/buying/localbuying.cfm. From here you will be able to search for programs by state and find out what type of first-time homebuyer programs and grants are available to you.

Before you get too deep into your home search, it's worth checking out what kind of programs are available to you. Make sure you check out all the different resources and find out what the benefits and downsides are to each program. No one program fits everyone, so it is important to do your homework and match these programs to your individual situation.

Once you've found a program that works for you, it's time to go shopping for a home.

7

How to Choose a Real Estate Partner

"From educating consumers about the housing market to supporting private property rights, Realtors enable more Americans to achieve and protect the dream of homeownership"
National Association of Realtors

Simply said, **<u>Don't do this by yourself</u>**. Don't make the largest financial transaction of your life alone or with someone that practices real estate occasionally. I have clients come to me all the time saying that their cousin or sister-in-law has their real estate license and practices real estate on the side. Let me ask you a question: would you go to a dentist that practiced dentistry "on the side"? Would you go to a lawyer that practiced law "on the side"? Then why use a real estate agent that practices real estate "on the side"? Statistics show that most people will by at least two (2) homes in their lifetime. If that is the case, you need to work with someone that practices real estate on a daily basis. To be successful at finding the perfect home for you, you need to partner yourself with professionals who have your interests in mind. Choosing the right real estate agent or broker is essential. You don't want to work with someone who just wants to sell you a house. You

want to work with someone who wants to sell you the right
house for you.

Furthermore, you want to work with a professional real
estate agent who is experienced and knows the area that you are
searching in well. You also want someone who has a good
understanding of the type of financing that you are looking for.
Many real estate agents work with local lenders on a regular
basis and buyers who have different credit needs. They can
steer you toward a lender who will be more favorable to your
unique situation, saving you time and aggravation when you go
to look for financing.

Here are some things to ask when choosing a real estate
agent or broker:

- How long have you been a real estate agent? Real
  estate agents have to go to school to become licensed.
  While a new real estate agent may be a bit hungrier
  on your behalf to find you the perfect home, you can't
  match the experience of an agent who has been
  working in the field for years. Every real estate agent
  needs to start with their first home. If that is you, it's
  best that you know this ahead of time so that you
  won't become frustrated if their inexperience causes
  you delays or problems. If you want someone who's
  experienced, look for a real estate agent who has been

working in the field for at least two years.

- <u>How many homes have you sold in the area in which I'm searching?</u> Remember, you want an agent that is knowledgeable about the area where you want to purchase a home. Beware of real estate brokers who say they can find you a home anywhere. It's not that they can't. In fact, a real estate broker can handle the transaction from anywhere in the world. But do you really want to work with a real estate broker from Boston if you're trying to find a home in Detroit?

- <u>Do you represent the buyer or seller? Or both?</u> There are some brokers that are known for being a Buyer's Agency. That means that instead of representing the interests of both the seller and the buyer to come up with a happy medium in selling a home, they will work solely on your behalf to get you the best deal they possibly can as the buyer.

- <u>Can I contact some people you have recently sold homes to in the area?</u> Most people are more than happy to give a reference when they have received good service. A good real estate agent will not be afraid to give you the names of a few references so you can find out if those buyers had any problems dealing with that agent.

- <u>Are you a full- or part-time real estate agent and what times are you available?</u> Many real estate agents work part-time to balance family and career. However, this could cause you problems if your schedules don't mesh. It's best to work with a real estate agent who works full-time and is available when you need him or her. If you can only look at homes on the weekends, make sure the real estate agent you choose is also available on the weekends to help you with your home search.

Nothing beats an informal chat with friends about who they have used in the past to help them find a home. Word-of-mouth goes a long way. In fact, most real estate agents count on that.

If someone has had a bad experience with a real estate agent you'll likely hear about that first. People are not as forthright with praise. But even if a friend has not talked about their experience with a real estate broker when they purchased their home, it can't hurt to ask about their experience. Ask them what they liked about their real estate agent and if there was anything they didn't like. Also, ask them if there is anything that they would do differently next time around.

Purchasing a home requires a professional who knows

the industry and knows the area you are looking in. There's a lot of complicated paperwork that goes into negotiating a deal. You want a professional who has the most experience to get you the best deal you can possibly get when purchasing a home.

Part 2: Building Generational Wealth: How to Turn Your 40 Acres into True Wealth!

8

Investing in More than Just Your 40 Acres

The quickest way to true wealth in America is by purchasing real estate. If you look over history and compare other forms of wealth-building, there is no other investment vehicle that provides a greater return than real estate. For years some of the wealthiest people in America have thrived due to their continued investments in real estate. Understanding how real estate can build wealth and create passive income is essential to tapping into this lucrative market share. We have spent the first part of this book showing you how to purchase your first home to live in. The last three chapters of this book will be devoted to truly showing you how to build wealth by purchasing investment real estate.

As you can remember earlier, my first real estate purchase was a duplex. I purchased in "da Hood" in Houston. The original reason I got into real estate was to be an investor. As a young man I noticed that there was wealth to be gained in real estate ownership. The duplex I purchased changed my life. I was able to sell that property for a huge profit and start my real estate business as well as purchase the family home that my wife and I live in. REAL ESTATE CAN CHANGE YOUR LIFE. So the question becomes, "How do you start the real estate investment process?"

WHAT TYPE OF REAL ESTATE INVESTOR DO YOU WANT TO BE?

Because I sell foreclosures for a living, I get hundreds of calls per year from first-time real estate investors. They usually have watched a TV show like *Flip That House* or *Flip This House* and they literally think that real estate investing is just like the show--that it only takes 30 minutes and you make a huge profit. Well that's not the case. There are some major decisions you have to make before you start looking for properties.

The first of those decisions is: what type of real estate investor are you or what type of investor do you want to be? The answer to this question is critical and that is why I ask it first. I use the example of stock investing. Stock investing is very similar to real estate investing in terms of risk considerations.

Here's a quick lesson in stock investing. There are many different risk categories for stock/mutual fund investing. There is **conservative investing** which typically includes very safe but low-yield bonds. There is **growth investing** or growth stocks where you are investing in companies that are undervalued and have a chance to appreciate or grow over time. There is also **dividend (or cash flow) investing** in which you invest in stocks or mutual funds that consistently pay their shareholders dividends. Finally, there is **speculation investing**. Speculation is essentially betting the market will go one way or the other-- up or down. You buy an investment vehicle like an option and you speculate which way the stock will go. Of course this is the riskiest form of investing. You can make way more money in speculative investing. However, the flip side of this is that you can lose ALL of your investment very quickly.

Taking these same terms, I can define the same risk categories in real estate investing. Conservative Real Estate Investing is purchasing real estate that may not provide the best initial return but has a good opportunity to provide a consistent return. If you are thinking you would like to invest but don't really want to deal with being a landlord or handling the other things that come with owning investment property, then this is for you. I will go over the types of real estate investments in more detail in the next chapter but a person that finds this investing style more appealing would probably be most comfortable investing in Real Estate Investment Trusts or through limited partnerships with active investors. With these types of investment vehicles, you do not have to be actively involved in the day-to-day operations of the property.

The next investing style that is available to beginning investors is <u>Growth Real Estate Investing</u>. With this style, you are more concerned about the appreciation of the property than you are the cash flow of the property. This is probably the riskiest form of real estate investing because you have to have the resources to purchase and renovate a property while at the same time paying the holding cost of owning the property.

<u>Cash Flow Real Estate Investing</u> is what I call the sweet spot of being a investor. EVERYONE should be a cash flow real estate investor. Why? I believe that the cash flow you derive from a property, with the right moves over time, can grow to provide a supplemental income that will ultimately make you rich. What is cash flow? Cash flow is the difference between your monthly cost to operate the property and the rents you derive from leasing the property. I believe that for beginning investors this amount should be NO LESS than $200 per month. That figure gives you enough room to actually save money over the course of ownership and use that money to either improve the property or save to buy additional properties. In Chapter 10 I will discuss my Millionaire real estate investment plan and a large part of that plan is to use the cash flow from the properties

to acquire more properties.

Let's spend some time talking about <u>Speculative Real Estate Investing.</u> This is the sexiest type of real estate investing; sexy in that it's the most tempting and possibly rewarding but also the most dangerous. Let me say this right now: DO NOT START YOUR REAL ESTATE INVESTMENT CAREER OFF WITH SPECULATION INVESTING. This type of investing has caused more heartaches for the beginning real estate investor than any other form of investing. As I stated earlier, speculation is a bet. The best example of this type of investing would be purchasing a property that is overpriced and has negative cash flow but you think it's in a "HOT" area that's going to have fast appreciation. The problem with that is that if you are a beginner and your bet on the area being "HOT" is wrong, you will own a property that is overpriced and costing you money every month. Most beginning investors don't have the resources to maintain speculative investment. I am not saying that you should never speculate. I just believe that you should wait until you are more experienced before entering into that type of investment.

Ideally the properties you identify will fit all three of these investing styles in one. They will be conservative, providing a safe and measurable return. They will provide growth in equity to cover the growth investment model. Most importantly again, they will provide cash flow, the single most important measure of a GOOD real estate investment.

OTHER CONSIDERATIONS WHEN PURCHASING MORE ACRES

Appreciation

Unlike many major purchases a person can make, real estate appreciates in value over time. In the last few years we have seen real estate prices skyrocket and then settle. One should never look at what is happening today in the real estate marketplace as a gauge for what will happen in the future, as the real estate market is always fluctuating.

One thing you can count on when you invest in real estate is that over the long haul the real estate you purchase will appreciate in value. This fact can give you much comfort when you invest because, unlike investments tied to stocks, you won't lose money with real estate unless you invest unwisely. The purpose of this book is to teach you how to invest wisely so that you build wealth, not lose money.

Historically, real estate values continue to increase in areas where there is high demand for properties. For instance, condominiums are very popular in highly populated urban areas. The price per square footage for these condominiums tends to be higher than the same size condominium in the suburbs of the city. But you won't lose money because condominiums continue to be in high demand for sale and for rent for urban dwellers.

The same is true for multifamily homes. There will always be a need for rental units as more people move to a city. Many first-time investors choose to live in one apartment and rent out the others to bring in income to help pay for their mortgage. Over time, as the balance of the loan is paid, the value of the home goes up. Because rents increase with inflation, eventually you could be living in your home rent-free while your tenants pay your mortgage.

If real estate is such a great deal--and it is--is there any reason to stop with purchasing just one home? From a financial standpoint the answer is no. The more real estate you invest in the more your net worth will continue to climb. How much you want your net worth to climb is up to you, but truly the sky's the limit.

If you do your homework right, check the real estate prices in the area and invest wisely; real estate is a relatively low-risk investment. <u>Emotion should never come into play when purchasing real estate</u>. Don't fall in love with a property. It's only real estate. It's not your girlfriend or boyfriend or a potential husband. If the numbers don't add up, or if the home you want to purchase is not going to bring you a profit, then you must walk away from it. There will always be another property to invest in.

Cash Flow

Another reason why real estate can help build wealth is that real estate can supply a steady source of what is known as passive income or cash flow as I discussed earlier. I mentioned earlier that some people purchase multifamily properties, live in one apartment and rent out the others. This can produce not only a way for you to live in a home rent-free, but also receive monthly monies as income. Let's look at the following example.

Say you find a three-family home or triplex that needs a little bit of cosmetic work and is selling for $200,000. It may cost $5,000 to fix it up and make it a nice place to live. Therefore, you can own a three-family home for approximately $205,000.

If the rents in the area are currently going for $750 per month and the mortgage payment plus taxes and insurance on the property equals $1,900 per month, you have yourself a winner! Let's look at the math:

Rent per unit $1,000 X 3 units	**$2,250.00**
Monthly Principal, Interest, Taxes and Insurance	**(-) $1,900.00**
Total amount of passive income at the end of the month	**$350.00**

If you decide to live in one of the apartments yourself and rent out the other two, your monthly payment each month will only be $400. This is not rent-free today, but as rental rates increase in the area and your mortgage payment stays the same, the amount you will need to pay per month will decrease and eventually the two other apartments will be paying for the entire mortgage.

Tax Advantages

Owning real estate also has significant tax advantages. When you rent a home all of the money that you pay for rent goes to the landlord to pay off their debt with the bank. The landlord can take all the tax write-offs that the federal government allows.

When you own real estate, you get those tax advantages. It is best to talk to a CPA who deals with real estate investing to make sure that you are taking advantage of the most tax write-offs that the law allows.

Increasing Your Property's Value

You don't need to own a home and just let it sit unchanged. There are many ways to increase the value of a property. For instance, updating the kitchen and bathroom, while costly, can improve the value of a home significantly.

Other things that add value are granite countertops, hardwood floors and landscaping. You can also replace older style cabinets or even add a few coats of fresh paint to the interior. These are just a few ways that you can improve the value of your home which will in turn generate more money for you when you sell. Keep in mind that you will pay taxes on the extra money you make when selling a property. Don't let this be a roadblock to you because there are ways to minimize taxes and maximize your net profit, as we will discuss. However, as an investor, consulting with your tax advisor is paramount.

Acquiring Investment Capital

There are different methods real estate investors use to acquire more money to invest in real estate. One way is to purchase a single-family home at a good price that needs a little sprucing up with the idea of increasing the value of the home so that you can refinance and take cash out. This is a very common tax-free method to acquire investment capital.

Let's say you purchase a home for $150,000. Putting $10,000 worth of work into sprucing it up can actually increase the value of the home to $200,000. Even before you sell the home, because its value has increased you have just made a profit of $40,000 on your investment. You can now do a cash-out refinance which is similar to a home equity loan. You will get a new mortgage on your home based on its new value of $200,000. However, since you only paid $160,000 for it ($150,000 plus the $10,000 you paid for renovations) you now have $40,000 equity in the home. So at closing, you can take home a check for a percentage of the $40,000 without having to pay Uncle Sam for the profit you would have made from selling the house. In other words, you can get up to $40,000 tax-free. Some lenders will only let you refinance up to 80% of the value of the home; however, some lenders will refinance for 100% of the value, allowing you to take all of the extra cash out.

You can do whatever you wish with the extra cash. You can invest in another property or you could simply put the cash in the bank for your own personal use. The choice is yours.

OVERCOMING FEAR

There are many ways you can build wealth with real estate. Unfortunately, many people become fearful of taking that first step. My acronym for F.E.A.R is False Evidence Appearing Real. Don't let the false evidence of what you have heard or someone else's horror story keep you from building wealth. Don't just spend your time "learning the process" and never practicing the method.

Another way people allow themselves to let fear keep them from investing in real estate is by spending too much time analyzing properties. While your property analysis is very important to make sure that you're getting the best deal you can get, don't allow yourself to get carried away to the point where that good deal is snatched out from under you by a quicker investor. You have to have a little courage to be a real estate investor. Sometimes all things aren't clear from the beginning. You have to trust that your methodologies are correct. If the property fits within your investment criteria then take a chance and go for it.

Taking that first step can be scary. But everyone who has invested in real estate and built wealth did it by buying that first house. So don't let your fear get in the way of you making a fortune in real estate. REMEMBER:

F.E.A.R = FALSE EVIDENCE APPEARING REAL!

9

Types of Real Estate to Look For When Investing

"Make your money going in!" That's what my mentor told me. You make a majority of your return in your initial negotiation. That is why the type of property you look for is so important. If you can get the right property at the right price you will hasten your quest to become a real estate millionaire. This is the premise I will use in the next chapter where I talk about my Guaranteed Millionaire Investor Plan. You have to purchase the property at the right price. How do you do that? First you need to work with your real estate professional to determine the values of an area. He will assist you in this by "running comps" which is providing you with information about comparable sales of similar properties. Then you look for properties that fall within your investment criteria which you have come up with after deciding what type of an investor you want to be as we discussed in the previous chapter. There are many different types of real estate to invest in to build wealth. Some are easier to get started in than others. However, some people do like to jump in with both feet. Don't let the ease or difficulty of any particular real estate deal be the criteria for deciding whether or not to purchase the property if you run the numbers and it looks like a good deal.

FORECLOSURES

Since 2005 I have had the contract in Southeast Texas to list all of the Government (HUD) foreclosures. I have listed and sold over 1,500 foreclosures since that time. I can tell you with a great degree of certainty that purchasing foreclosures is the easiest way for you to build wealth through real estate. Essentially you are purchasing a property in a distressed state that, because it's a foreclosure, you still have time to do your due diligence on as pertains to price, condition, market rents, etc. Foreclosures are for both the experienced investor and the new investor. They can be for the investment group as well. Currently, there are more foreclosures on the market right now than there have been in the last 20 or 30 years. It is a sad fact but one that you can take advantage of to help you build wealth through real estate.

Let's get this out of the way first. Some people find profiting from another person's hard times unsettling. Shouldn't we want to help people who are in trouble? That is a noble thing to feel and to do. However, the people who have their houses foreclosed on were in trouble long before you came upon the scene. There is no way that you can help everyone who has been hurt by a foreclosure. If you don't purchase their home, some other investor will, so why shouldn't it be you? Remember this as well, if you purchase a foreclosure and either sell it to a nice family or put a good family in it to rent you are winning on both sides. Economically you are, hopefully, getting a good return on your investment. Morally you are helping to build neighborhoods with strong families. So don't feel guilty about purchasing foreclosures.

The benefit of purchasing a foreclosed home is that you'll be able to buy the house at a reduced rate. The circumstances surrounding the original mortgage and how much is owed can determine how much the bank is willing to give the house up for. However, in some markets, investors are able to purchase homes at 30%, 40% or even 50% off the market price.

WAYS TO PURCHASE FORECLOSURES

There are three different ways to purchase a foreclosure. They are:

1. Prior to the Foreclosure Auction
2. At the Foreclosure Auction
3. From an REO Broker/Agent

Prior to the Foreclosure Auction

Technically, if you purchase a property prior to the foreclosure auction then it's really not a foreclosure. I talk about this type of purchase here because in the industry we call this a pre-foreclosure. Depending on the numbers, this can be the best time to purchase an investment property. It is the best time due to the fact you are dealing with the original owner and their mortgage company and there is no "go-between". As you can tell from the proliferation of "We Buy Houses" signs that splatter most neighborhoods, purchasing a property in a "distress" situation can get you a very good return on your investment dollar.

On a typical pre-foreclosure sale, you are purhasing a home that the owner can no longer afford. So instead of letting the home go into foreclosure most home owners will try to sell it. Why would they do this? Because most of them want to become homeowners again, and having a foreclosure on their credit report will keep them from purchasing a home for at least a year, if not more. So the good thing is that you are dealing with a motivated seller.

Here is what you need to look out for so that you don't get burned in this process. Because you are purchasing a home in pre-foreclosure you have to be aware that the person you are purchasing it from has gone through or is going through financial problems. That means that there may be other liens against the property besides the mortgage. So, if you find an opportunity like this, make sure that you are working with a title professional to make sure that there are no other liens (i.e., IRS tax liens, judgments, family claims, etc.) that are attached to the deed. So remember, if you can develop a system of getting consistent "pre-foreclosure" leads, I recommend this as a great area to start in.

At the Foreclosure Auction

If you are not lucky enough to get a home prior to foreclosure then the next best place is at the foreclosure auction. The foreclosure auction I am referring to is the initial one conducted by a trustee on behalf of the bank. In most counties in America, there is a designated day of the month where foreclosure auctions occur. For example, in Texas, on the first Tuesday of every month at the steps of every county courthouse, there is a foreclosure auction. You will need to check with your city, county, parish or state government to see when this happens in your area.

Here is the great thing about this auction: all of these properties will go to the highest bidder. That's right, if you bid the highest the house is yours. That sounds great but again be careful and do your research. These properties sometimes still have other non-real estate liens that have not been cleared. So again, it would be smart to work with a title company to make sure, prior to the auction, that you have a clean title. In addition to title issues, since these properties are still typically occupied by their owners, you do not typically get to view and inspect them. That is another risk you bear if you purchase investment property at the foreclosure auction.

Another difference in this type of auction is that in most states you have to have all of your money when you win the bid. This option keeps most beginning investors out. You heard me correctly, if you win a bid at $150,000, you need to have $150,000 in cash or certified funds right there to claim your prize. I highly recommend that you become an experienced investor before you invest at a foreclosure auction. I have seen many a beginning investor lose all they have trying to start out at a foreclosure auction of this kind.

From an REO Broker/Agent

First let me define REO for you. REO refers to "Real Estate Owned." This is how banks refer to properties that they have in their inventory. Banks are in the money business, NOT the real estate business. As soon as a loan has defaulted (foreclosed) they have real estate that they own. If it is not sold at the real estate auction discussed above then the responsibility of selling that property is given to a real estate broker that specializes in selling foreclosures. That's what my business is focused on. We specialize in listing and selling real estate foreclosures.

I can tell you firsthand that purchasing property at this stage, what I call post-foreclosure, can be rewarding if done correctly. Lesson #1 when purchasing at this stage is to know that the bank is typically trying to get maximum dollar for the property. Sometimes banks will list properties at lower prices initially if the property has more work that needs to be done to it than they are willing to do. However, my experience has been that if the property is in good shape the lender will sometimes try to get market value. Lesson #2 when buying at this stage is that the longer the property has been on the market the more flexibility there is from the bank's standpoint to negotiate. Again, experience has taught me that if a property has been on the market for more than 90 days, the BANK WANTS TO GET RID OF IT. So my suggestion is to MAKE AN OFFER!

MULTIFAMILY HOMES

Multifamily homes can be anything from a duplex with two apartments to an apartment building or series of apartment buildings with many units. Multifamily property investing is very lucrative for the real estate investor. As the mortgage on the property is paid down and the cost of rent goes up, the investor makes a passive income. Investing in multifamily properties the right way can yield you enough monthly income to live on so that you can go from being a 9-to-5 employee at your day job to an independent real estate investor building wealth.

The benefit of purchasing multifamily properties is that they are plentiful. People have to live somewhere, and not all people can afford or even want to purchase their own home. This is where you solve their problem, give them a nice apartment to live in, and they in turn pay you rent. The more multifamily properties you purchase, the more passive income you'll accumulate.

COMMERCIAL PROPERTIES

Like multifamily properties, commercial properties are available on every street corner. The corner grocery store, gas station, doctor's office, law office, or industrial park could all be commercial buildings for an investor to invest in.

There are advantages to purchasing commercial real estate that are unlike those of other types of real estate. For instance, the leases tend to be long-term. This saves you a lot of the aggravation of trying to find new tenants every few months which sometimes happens with residential properties. On the downside, you might also have long vacancies until you find the right business to lease the space. Working with a good commercial real estate leasing agent will help a lot towards keeping your properties leased with good tenants.

LEASE/OPTION

A wonderful way to get started in purchasing real estate is to use the lease with option to buy strategy. This is particularly helpful if you do not have a lot of money to put down on a home.

When you lease a home with an option to buy it, part of the monthly rent is set aside and put towards a down payment for when the lessee purchases the home. Most lease with option to purchase contracts generally go from one to two years, as most sellers do not want to tie up their property forever.

If at the end of two years the lessee decides he or she wants to purchase the property, the portion of the money that was set aside is then applied as their down payment on the house. This gives them those two years to save money for closing costs, repairs, or additional money to put down on the property.

For instance, if you lease a property to someone for $1,000 per month and write in the contract that $200 per month will be applied toward the purchase price, at the end of two years they will have a down payment of $4,800. That is equal to the 3% down payment needed for an FHA loan on a $160,000 house. The more money per month you can negotiate going towards the purchase price of the home, the better.

LAND

A common phrase you may have heard is, "They're not making any more land." But that doesn't mean that you can't profit from the land that's available. Some investors choose to focus their attention on open land. They purchase acreage and then subdivide it for a higher amount per acre than what they bought it for.

10

The 40 Acre Millionaire Maker!!
"Don't Believe the Hype!" – Public Enemy

I know you've heard it before. You've been watching TV
or listening to the radio and you have heard the hype man say
he has the perfect real estate plan for you to make millions with
NO MONEY DOWN or WITH NO EXPERIENCE. Well like one
of my favorite rap groups, Public Enemy says, "Don't Believe
the Hype." Making millions in real estate takes time. Are there
people who get lucky and do it faster than others do? Yes.
However, I would guess that would be less than 1% of the
people who actively invest in real estate. Don't get caught up in
the GET RICH QUICK real estate investment guys on TV. Ask
yourself this: are they making more money selling you their
"secret" or buying and selling real estate?

So how do you do it? How do you start the process of
making millions in real estate? I've got the plan for you. I call it
the 40 ACRE MILLONAIRE MAKER!! That's right. This plan,
if followed as laid out below, will allow you to develop a
million dollar net worth within 5 to 10 years of investing.

Step 1: Identify Millionaire Maker Properties

This is the most important step in the process. You have to identify the correct Millionaire Maker Property. What is a Millionaire Maker Property? Here are the criteria:

- **The property must have Immediate Equity!** THIS IS THE MOST IMPORTANT CHARACTERISTIC OF A MILLIONAIRE MAKER PROPERTY. The property must have at least 20% equity at the time you purchase it. That's right, 20%. If it does not, MOVE ON. If you do not adhere to this, everything else I tell you from here on out is worthless.

  You are looking for properties that can be purchased for 80% of their market value. How would you know this? Because you have put your team together: your real estate professional, mortgage professional, tax advisor and if necessary (as with foreclosures) title professional. Your real estate professional has provided you with comparable sales of similar properties and both of you have determined what the market value of the property is.

  Here's a numbers example. Let's say you identify a single family home that is listed for sale at $80,000. Your realtor provides you with three (3) comparable properties in the same neighborhood that sold for $105k, $100k, and $98k. Does this fit our "Immediate Equity" Formula? If we take the average of the comparables above we get an average Sold price of $101,000. Dividing $80,000 by $101,000 we get 80%. Therefore this property would fit our "Immediate Equity" formula. Now let's say this same property needs $5000 worth of repairs. Does it still meet our criteria? No. This would take us over our 80% requirement. You can, however, negotiate into our formula. You may be able to make an offer for $75,000 and therefore have the seller "eat" the cost of repairs. You could also negotiate the seller doing the repairs with a full price $80,000 offer. Just remember that no matter what... **The property must have immediate equity.**

- **The property must be rentable**. I know that sounds easy but I also know that first-time investors will go out and find "deals" where they have to do too much work. Here is what you need to ask yourself, "Is this a carpet and paint property?" Carpet and paint properties are ones that need very few upgrades to make them rentable. You also need to ask yourself whether this property is the appropriate size, the appropriate shape, in a decent area, etc. All of these factors come into play when purchasing your property.

- **The property must have positive rental cash flow**. Why? Because with my Millionaire Maker plan you will be holding this property for a while and it does not make good financial sense to have an investment property that is costing you money every month. How will you know if it will have positive cash flow? Again, you will use your team. Your realtor can provide rental comparables for the area. Your mortgage lender/broker can provide you with what your monthly cost will be. If you are able to rent the property for more than you are paying for the property than you have a positive rental cash flow. NOTE: With single family homes, I personally like to net at least $200 per month. Depending on your market this may be low or high. However, I think you should NOT be in a situation where your rent is the same as your monthly mortgage payment.

So we have our criteria: the property must have Immediate Equity, the property must be rentable, the property must have positive rental cash flow. These criteria are fundamental to real estate investing. Even if you have no desire to become a real estate millionaire, if you stick to these criteria you will never go wrong.

Now that we have our criteria let's look at **The 40 Acre Millinaire Maker 5 Year Plan:**

Years 1 – 5: The Accumulation Period

During years 1 through 5 of our plan, you are accumulating properties. More specifically, you are purchasing at least one (1) property per year that fits our criteria. I always get the question, "Can't I purchase more if I want to or I see more opportunities?" The answer is YES. The only reason I say one (1) is that is the MINIMUM you need. A word of caution, though: don't overextend yourself financially or physically. Identifying property can be intoxicating. There is a real natural high that comes with building lasting wealth. However, you don't want to purchase too many properties too fast. If you do, you could overextend yourself financially. You could also overextend yourself physically. Remember, you will be managing the day-to-day responsibilities of being a landlord. The hope is that you are purchasing properties that don't need any maintenance. Unfortunately though, even the best properties need work now and then.

Just make sure that during the accumulation period you stick to what's financially and physically comfortable for you.

For most of my clients that are not full-time real estate investors, one home per year is just the right pace.

Year 6: The Upgrade Period

Beyonce' has a song called "Upgrade" where she talks about upgrading her boyfriend if he does not act right. Well Year 6 of the 40 Acre Millionaire Maker is the year we are upgrading our properties. Let's review where we are. If you followed the criteria and rules above, your real estate portfolio should look something like the table below:

Property	[1]Purchase Price	[1]Value at time of Purchase	[2]Current Market Value	Monthly Cash Flow
Property #1	$80,000	$100,000	$121,550	$200
Property #2	$80,000	$100,000	$115,762	$200
Property #3	$80,000	$100,000	$110,250	$200
Property #4	$80,000	$100,000	$105,000	$200
Property #5	$80,000	$100,000	$100,000	$200
TOTALS:			$552,562	$1,000

Assumptions: 1. I used the same purchase price and value for each property. I did this to emphasize how critical it is that the Immediate Equity Formula is used. 2. On average, real estate appreciates (goes up in value) every year by 5%. I assumed that this would continue to be the case and therefore used 5% appreciation in this example. FINAL NOTE: In the table above I made no attempt to estimate what would still be owed on each mortgage since each investor would be making different decisions as to rate, down payment and program.

Let me say this before I continue with the plan: if after five (5) years you have a real estate portfolio that looks like the table above and you decide not to follow the rest of the steps I will outline, you are already on your way to owning real estate that will be valued at more than one million dollars over the next 10 years. If you take the Current Market Value Total calculated above and use our 5% appreciation assumption, these properties will cumulatively increase in value to OVER one million dollars! Just by following the steps outlined above and going no further you would be in the top 5% of real estate investors over time.

Now, how do you UPGRADE? You take each of the properties above and you SELL THEM!! That's right!! Working with your team you sell each of them for their current market value! Why? Because you are going to use the equity you have in each property and purchase your ultimate 40 Acre Millionaire Maker PROPERTY! Let's see how the numbers would work if you SOLD each of the properties above:

Property	[1]Purchase Price	[2]Current Market Value	Net Equity
Property #1	$80,000	$121,550	**$41,550**
Property #2	$80,000	$115,762	**$35,762**
Property #3	$80,000	$110,250	**$30,250**
Property #4	$80,000	$105,000	**$25,000**
Property #5	$80,000	$100,000	**$20,000**
TOTALS:		$552,562	**$152,562**

This is so powerful. As you can see from the table above you would have $152,562 dollars to invest if you sold the properties. WOW!! That's the power of real estate. There is no other investment vehicle that would give you that return over the same amount of time.

The question becomes how do you turn $152K into a million? You use that money to UPGRADE to a large multifamily and/or commercial property! That's it! I wish it were more complicated than that. Why a large apartment complex or commercial property? They self-manage, pure and simple. Self manage means they generate enough income to pay staff or a management company to manage them so you don't have to. In addition and most importantly, these properties typically have MILLION DOLLAR MARKET VALUATIONS, thereby making you a 40 ACRE MILLIONAIRE!!!

That's the plan. In a nutshell, purchase 5 single family homes over 5 years using my criteria, sell them at the end of the 5 years and upgrade to a large apartment building or commercial property (remembering that the criteria does not change when you go to apartment buildings or commercial properties--these properties still have to follow the fundamentals from above).

<u>NEXT STEPS?!?!</u>

If you have already purchased your own home as discussed in
Part 1 of the book, then there is no time like the present to start
the 40 ACRE MILLIONAIRE MAKER plan. Be Diligent. Be
Disciplined. And most importantly--have faith in yourself and
your abilities.

The Last Acre...

Having a home to call your own is the right of every human being, no matter who they are or where they live. As an African-American people we have struggled through oppression, gained freedom, and can now take our place in the financial world of building wealth through real estate where once it was only a dream.

Anyone of any race or creed can become a homeowner if he or she has the knowledge to do so. In this book, you've been given the tools that you need to go out and not only purchase the home of your dreams for you and your family, but also to go beyond merely owning real estate to live in. You've been given a blueprint to build wealth through investing in real estate to give you security and allow you to live a life you may have only dreamed of.

As with any new step a person makes in life, investing in your first home or your first investment property can be scary. I know this because I've been there. Take comfort in knowing that every person who has invested in real estate for wealth has started in the same place you are in right now. They started with the first property. And so can you.

Don't allow your fear to get in the way of taking that first step. Once you do and you feel comfortable with the process, you will have more confidence and you will begin to set goals for yourself beyond what you've seen in this book.

Truly, the sky is the limit. Only you can hold yourself back and only you can reach as high as you can go. I wish you luck and good fortune in building your real estate portfolio.

About Kevin Riles

Kevin Riles, a native of Houston, Texas, received a
Bachelor of Science degree in Computer Science with cum laude
honors from Morehouse College in 1995. Kevin attended
Morehouse College on a full $75,000 Ronald E. McNair NASA
Scholarship, due to his academic accomplishments at
Willowridge High School in Houston, Texas. With its tradition
of producing leaders, Morehouse helped Kevin tap his
leadership potential. As a further testament to Kevin's
academic achievements, he received his Masters of Business
Administration in Finance from the University of Saint Thomas
in July of 2000. Kevin is currently working on his PhD in
Business at the prestigious International School of Business
based in Paris, France.

Kevin began his professional career as a systems analyst
with ExxonMobil. During his business career Kevin has worked
for ExxonMobil Corporation, Clear Channel Communications
(KMJQ 102.1 FM) and Managed Information Systems. His
wide array of business experience, coupled with his strong
entrepreneurial desires caused him to form Quest Capital
Mortgage and Upscale Properties in October of 2000 to provide
mortgage financing and real estate brokerage services to the
Greater Houston Area. In May 2006, Kevin purchased a
RE/MAX franchise and is now the broker/owner of RE/MAX

Upscale Properties. Kevin is also the Branch Manager for Southwest Funding, a full service mortgage banker with corporate headquarters in Dallas, TX.

In 2005, Kevin was named the Broad Listing Broker for HUD Foreclosures in the greater Houston Area. With this contract he has responsibility for listing HUD foreclosures in an eighteen-county area. In 2006, Kevin SOLD 604 Homes! He has sold over 160 million dollars worth of properties! He is expected to list over 1000 foreclosures a year over the next 5 years. With his team of experienced Mortgage Consultants and Real Estate Agents, his company is well-positioned to live up to its mission: "Excellence in Real Estate." He is committed to educating people on the benefits of homeownership and especially helping first-time homebuyers with access to capital.

Kevin is also a highly sought-after motivational speaker. He has hosted his own radio show on Business Radio 650 in Houston entitled, "Real Estate Matters with Kevin Riles." He has motivated people on his views of success at corporations and organizations such as ExxonMobil, INROADS Houston, Fort Bend Independent School District, CAN Academy and many others. Kevin's "Tools and Formula for Success" have inspired countless adults and youth to reach for a higher purpose.

Kevin is also a proud member of the National Association of Real Estate Brokers (NAREB), National Association of Realtors (NAR) and Alpha Phi Alpha Fraternity, Inc.

Kevin's mission in life is to positively impact the lives of people socially, economically and spiritually. With the help of God, and his supportive and beautiful wife Cher and daughter Madison, Kevin will realize his mission.

To find out more information on Kevin or to have him speak to your organization on Real Estate, Success and Motivation, please contact his office at the numbers below:

Kevin Riles
2938 South Main
Stafford, TX 77477
Phone: (281) 403-3700
Email: info@kevinriles.com
Website:
http://www.KevinRiles.com

NOTES:

NOTES:

NOTES:

www.ingramcontent.com/pod-product-compliance
Lightning Source LLC
Chambersburg PA
CBHW031212270326
41931CB00006B/539